THE CUP

How the 2006 Ryder Cup Was Won

Published in 2006 by Maverick House Publishers.

Maverick House, Main Street, Dunshaughlin, Co. Meath, Ireland.
Maverick House SE Asia, 440 Sukhumvit Road, Washington Square,
Klongton, Klongtoey, Bangkok 10110, Thailand.

www.maverickhouse.com
email: info@maverickhouse.com

ISBN: 978-1-905379-24-8 (1-905379-24-2)

Printed and bound by Colourbooks Ltd.

5 4 3 2 1

The paper used in this book comes from wood pulp of managed forests.
For every tree felled at least one tree is planted, thereby renewing natural
resources.

A CIP catalogue record for this book is available from the British Library.

THE CUP

How the 2006 Ryder Cup Was Won

PHILIP REID

DEDICATION

To my sons, Conor and Evan;
two great caddies.

Contents

ACKNOWLEDGEMENTS

Anyone who knows Malachy Logan, the sports editor of *The Irish Times,* will be aware that when he puts a germ of an idea into your head, it is not something easily dismissed. So, I suppose I had better start by thanking him for planting the seed for this book and believing that I was the right man to see it through.

I would also like to wholeheartedly thank the team at Maverick House Publishers, particularly John Mooney and Adam Hyland, for giving this book the same commitment that I did in recording what was a momentous occasion not just for Ireland, but in world terms, in 2006.

As golf writers, we in the profession know that we are fortunate to deal with players who, in the main, are articulate and approachable. Long may that continue, and my thanks go to them. Also, I would like to thank the media department on the PGA European Tour—particularly Gordon Simpson, Scott Crockett and Mitchell Platts—and Julius Mason, of the PGA of America, for their invaluable assistance throughout a long year for everyone.

To Ray McManus and his team at Sportsfile, thanks for the images. To Helen Newman, for your encouragement and belief, and to Kay and Jackie, my parents, who have always supported me; thanks.

Finally, but not least, to my two boys, Conor and Evan, who wondered why Dad continued to spend more hours in front of the laptop than on the course (wishful thinking) or kicking football even when the Ryder Cup had finished. This is why. I hope it is worth it. Thanks.

Philip Reid, October 2006.

INTRODUCTION

IT IS ONLY VERY OCCASIONALLY that those of us on the outside of professional sport get a true insight into that elite world. I have always liked Ernie Els and, a few years ago, I could have hugged him when he drew my name out of a hat or crystal bowl—who knows?—and earned me an invite to play in the Dunhill Links championship, a fully-fledged tournament on the PGA European Tour. It was 2002.

Originally, my pro-am partner was due to be Alex Cejka, a German player making a good fist of moving up the world rankings at that time but, unfortunately, prone to occasional back injuries. That week, Cejka was forced to cry off, quite late, and Chris Gane, an affable fledgling English tour player battling to retain his tour card for the following season, replaced him.

I remember my first tee shot on the first day of the Dunhill Links. It was on the Old Course at St Andrews and my knees were literally shaking like jelly. I had been to the revered links on numbers of occasions to cover tournaments for *The Irish Times* but never played it. This was a dream come true. Ivor Robson, the starter, had introduced me—to a smattering of applause, believe it or not—and, suddenly, I was away over the famed humps and hollows, with a bagman who had 17 years of experience at guiding golfers over the links.

On the Par 5 fifth hole, reality hit home in a big way. After a decent drive and a somewhat intelligent lay-up with a five-iron, I was left with 134 yards to the green. Of course, the third shot never went close to finding it. Richard, my caddie, was not impressed.

'Do you know, that is the biggest green in the world,' he said of the green that doubled with the 13th. 'It measures one and a half acres, and you've managed to miss it with a nine-iron.' His displeasure couldn't have been worse if Nick Faldo had taken the shot.

Needless to say, as a team, Chris and myself failed to make the top 20 who survived to play into the fourth and final day. Sadly for Chris, he failed to make the cut in the individual tournament, which was won by Padraig Harrington, and failed to keep his card for the following season. A bigger insight into the distress of those who had been in a similar plight to that of Chris came when we entered the locker room of the clubhouse at Kingsbairns on that third and, for us, final day's play. Chris limited himself to an anguished roar, of frustration I guessed. Others had not been so restrained. Littered all around the room were broken putter shafts.

Very few of those golfers who get to play in the Ryder Cup get to experience such levels of frustration, where one putt can literally mean having something to eat and not. Yet, if it is any inspiration for fledgling professionals, or those daring to dream the dream, many of those who made it to the 2006 Ryder Cup match at The K Club had struggled in their early playing days. And this applied to the two captains, Europe's Ian Woosnam and the United States' Tom Lehman, more than most.

Woosnam had needed three visits to the European Tour qualifying school before finding his feet on tour. Before that, he had played the Safari Circuit in Africa where he used to travel in a camper van, and meet his eating needs by surviving on tins of beans. He was to rise to become world number one, and a US Masters champion.

Likewise, Tom Lehman didn't find it easy to make it, initially, on to the PGA Tour. He became a global player and competed on the Asian Tour and on the secondary and third-tier tours in America before he found his feet. So strapped for cash had he been as he struggled to make any impact, Lehman had spent the early 1990s travelling from one tournament venue to another in a battered old car with 180,000 miles on the clock. His perseverance paid off: in a second lease of life on the PGA Tour, hardened by what he had endured on the road, he developed into one of the game's great players. The highpoint came when he won the British Open in 1996.

Back in those early days of struggling on tour, neither Woosnam nor Lehman could ever have envisaged playing, never mind captaining, teams in the Ryder Cup. But their talent eventually came through, and they arrived at The K Club as the leaders of two teams' intent on making the 36th edition of the tournament the greatest ever. Of the 24 players who arrived in Ireland with the captains, 20 of them had successfully come through qualifying campaigns. The other four had been the captains' 'wild card' selections.

The United States qualifying entailed a two-year system loaded to the second half of the campaign, in the belief that in-form players would make the team. The result was a side that featured the top-three players in the official world golf rankings, but which also featured four rookies: Vaughn Taylor, Zach Johnson, JJ Henry and Brett Wetterich.

The European qualifying covered two different methods of qualifying. The top five players were selected from a world points list based on world ranking points won over a one-year campaign, with the next five players qualifying from a European points list with earnings (one euro equalling one point) from counting events on the PGA European Tour, again over one year. It was a system devised to enable players mainly based on the PGA Tour to qualify without requiring a captain's pick. As far as Team Europe was concerned, it was a system that had much going for it.

·   ·   ·   ·

THE RYDER CUP HAD STARTED out as nothing more than a gentlemen's match between professional golfers from the United States and Great Britain when it was first staged in 1927. For many years, it was simply an excuse for American golfers to reaffirm their superiority over their British contemporaries. The remit for the British team was extended to include Irish players, one of whom, Christy O'Connor, went on to play in ten matches. But, more often than not, the result was the same: United States winning, Great Britain and Ireland losing.

It all changed when Jack Nicklaus, the greatest player of his era, and a man with a record 18 majors to his name, effectively said that enough was enough. Even the great ones get tired of winning too easily and it was he who suggested that the net should be extended to include continental European players. So it was that Team Europe came about, and, in golf, Europe's sporting nations found a common bond. The arrival of Seve Ballesteros *et al* transformed the Ryder Cup.

In truth, nobody, not even Nicklaus, could have envisaged that the Ryder Cup would change as much as it did. It became the most white-knuckle ride in golf, with even major winners admitting to feeling nerves and wobbly knees and barely able to see the ball when standing on the first tee at a Ryder Cup for the first time.

When Tom Lehman brought his 12 men to the K Club, his team were tasked with seeking to become the first from the United States to avoid a third successive defeat in the competition.

Europe's goal was entirely different. Ian Woosnam's team— which included Darren Clarke, playing on a captain's 'wild card' pick just six weeks after the death of his wife, Heather—were attempting to become the first European side to win three Ryder Cups in a row.

Prior to the match, Woosnam had expressed the heartfelt feeling that the 2006 Ryder Cup would be a 'beacon to fair play, intense competition and magnanimity.' He had also suggested that he would require a 'back door' out if Europe failed to win, so passionate was the Irish golfing public. The scene was set for what promised to be a magnificent sporting event, and it did not disappoint. This is the story of how the Ryder Cup 2006 was won.

ONE

Calm before the Storm

Dublin, Ireland. January 2006.

THE SKYLINE OF DUBLIN'S DOCKLANDS bore testimony to a changing city; a backdrop of towering cranes where office blocks and apartments replace old gasworks and warehouses at a pace unprecedented in the city's long and rich history.

One cool morning, in the very early days of a new year, a man who was instantly recognisable to those gathered on the dockside emerged from one of those new company headquarters that have sprouted up along the River Liffey, the waterway that runs through Ireland's capital city.

The man was holding a gold trophy and, as he left the offices of communications company O_2 and walked across the road at Sir John Rogerson's Quay, the sight of the Ryder Cup in Padraig Harrington's hands was enough to literally bring all quayside traffic to a standstill.

Cars were abandoned by the side of the road, drivers leaving them so that they could crowd around, uninvited, on the photo shoot that had the golfer cradling the most cherished trophy in international team golf as if it were a newborn baby.

His pose was that of a protective guardian, unwilling to let the cherished cup, with the likeness of Abe Mitchell—an artisan turned professional golfer—at its apex, leave his grasp.

Suddenly, the crowd of onlookers swelled. Those who had deserted their vehicles were joined by a number of naval personnel who had vacated the Irish Navy's flagship vessel, the *LE Eithne*, docked nearby and scheduled to leave shortly afterwards on a transatlantic trip to Argentina to honour Admiral William Brown, the Irish-born founder of that country's navy.

The crowd got steadily larger, as still others deserted their morning coffees to join the throng. It was a remarkable scene.

Through it all, all of this gentle madness and organised mayhem, Harrington, stood by the waterside, wearing his trademark grin. Inside, you wonder, was his stomach churning? If the mere presence of the Ryder Cup on a quayside nine months before the encounter between Europe and the United States was sufficient to cause such a reaction, what would it be like at the actual match?

For Harrington, an Irish sporting icon, the craziness of this scene on the dockside was not unexpected. He knew how the Irish, more than any other nation, idolised sporting heroes. He knew that each one of those gathered on this dockside expected him to be a part of the Ryder Cup. He also knew that, on that day in January, he was far from assured of a place on the European Team. He knew he had a lot of catching up to do if he was to qualify. There was much work to be done.

· · · ·

PADRAIG HARRINGTON'S YOUNG SON, PATRICK, was watching children's television. Power Rangers. The doorway from the TV room to the kitchen was open and Harrington's wife, Caroline, was manoeuvring a wok on the cooker while keeping an eye on her child. She emptied a sachet of fresh noodles into the pan and, with a sense of perfect timing, Harrington arrived to take a stool at the counter. Lunch was served.

When lunch—finished off with ice cream—was over, Harrington led the way downstairs to the basement which houses a personal gym with all the latest equipment and a games room with snooker table and pinball machine, among other things, to keep his mind occupied. Also in this part of the house is an office whose shelves are lined with books; History, Sport, Biographies; but mainly History.

In the safety of his neat and tidy office in his home in Rathmichael in the foothills of the Dublin mountains, Harrington—a member of Europe's Ryder Cup team in 1999, 2002 and 2004—was in Ryder Cup mode, even if the match itself was months away and he had some work to do before he was guaranteed a place on the team.

'I've a lot to do to qualify, to get in the team,' acknowledged Harrington who, at that moment in time, was 13th in the world points list and 12th in the European points list, the two means of obtaining an automatic place on Ian Woosnam's team.

As things stood, Harrington was not yet on the team. But he knew that the 2006 season was about more than the match, adding: 'If all I did this year was make the Ryder Cup team, it would obviously be a disappointing year.'

He sat back in his leather chair as the 17th ranked player in the official world golf rankings. At one point in 2004, he had reached as high a ranking as sixth. He sat there as a player who delayed a move into the professional ranks so that he could complete his accountancy studies.

· · · ·

AS A YOUNG BOY GROWING up, Harrington had demonstrated terrific sporting ability. His father, Paddy, who died in July of 2005, just days before the British Open at St Andrews, had played in two Gaelic Football All-Ireland Finals in the 1950s with his native Cork. His son Padraig inherited some of that footballing acumen. He even captained his school team in a final in Croke Park, where an encounter with a young, blonde footballer from Glasnevin called Dessie Farrell confirmed that his future lay in golf and not Gaelic Football.

Another story goes that, one time, he went on a school trip to New York to play football and came back with a cup for Irish dancing. The cultural input, it seems, came from his mother, Breda. Michael Flatley was not to have anything to fear, however. Life on stage was not something that Harrington would pursue.

Instead, it was the golfing bug that infiltrated his sporting psyche more than any other. His dad, a policeman, was one of the founding members of Stackstown Golf Club in the foothills of the Dublin Mountains and it was here that the young Padraig was first introduced, at the age of four, to the sport that was to become his livelihood. He represented Ireland at all levels in amateur golf, building a reputation as a gritty competitor; a player who knew the importance of getting the ball into the hole in as few strokes as possible.

The young Harrington was always seen as ultra-competitive, which was no bad thing. Whether it was competing at marbles on the streets outside his home in Rathfarnham, or on the football pitch or, especially, on the golf course, Harrington always wanted to win.

It's a trait that was inbuilt by being the youngest of five brothers.

As an amateur golfer, Harrington got his first taste of playing against the United States when selected on the Great Britain and Ireland team for the Walker Cup match in 1991. He was to play in the match again in 1993 and 1995; but the 1991 match was different. Not only was it his debut, the match was played in Portmarnock, a links course on Dublin's northern coastline. The match attracted record numbers of spectators and, although the

United States won, Harrington was given an early foretaste of what such spectacles meant to the golfing public.

Times have changed for Harrington in the decade and a half since he first donned the Great Britain & Ireland sweater and faced a team that included Phil Mickelson on the links at Portmarnock. He was 24, a fully qualified accountant, when he made the move. If he took his time ascending into the professional ranks, it didn't take him long to make an impact. When he won his first cheque at a tournament in South Africa, a sum equivalent to about €1,800, he phoned home to tell his parents that they 'were giving money away.'

Weeks later, in his ninth tournament of his rookie season on the PGA European Tour in 1996, Harrington won the Spanish Open. From someone who had joined the tour content to be little more than a journeyman, he had raised the bar for himself; and also raised his expectations and that of others. He had moved from the shadows into the sun, and life for him would never be the same again.

His swing was never a classic one. When he turned to Bob Torrance, father of Sam, to be his coach, the old Scot was amazed.

'When I first saw Padraig, his technique was poor. His swing didn't create a lot of leverage and his lower body movement was awful. He had a very flat shoulder plane and a deep arm swing … ach, his swing was awful!,' Torrance would later say.

But, in Harrington, Torrance had found a pupil who worked harder than anyone else in the game. He was willing to undergo a transformation of his technique, willing to put in endless hours on the practice ground at tournaments around the world; and willing to fly over from his home in Dublin to Torrance's home in Largs on the west coast of Scotland so that his swing would be one capable of standing up to the pressures and demands of winning the very top tournaments. Torrance, who himself doesn't know when it is time to stop working, had found the ideal student.

In his time as a professional golfer, Harrington has made hard calls. Switching coaches from Howard Bennett to Torrance, changing caddies from Dave McNeilly to Ronan Flood, opting to use a drive off the 18th hole in the 2003 British Open at Muirfield; he did what he thought was best for him. And that's the bottom line. He possessed an inner steel.

· · · ·

As HARRINGTON RESTED HIS ELBOWS on the desk in his office on that January afternoon, he did so as Ireland's highest profile international sportsman. In his time competing as a professional on the golf courses of the world, he has won 15 tournaments and accumulated in excess of €16 million in prize money. He has also racked up a disproportionate number of runner-up finishes but, hey, worse things could happen in life.

He has done well. He has a beautiful wife; a lovely child; a fine house in the Dublin foothills, with his own short game practice area and a number of golf holes that he himself designed.

Golf itself is a selfish sport, but the Ryder Cup—two teams, 12 men from Europe against 12 men from the United States—is different. Players bond, competing not only for themselves, but for entire continents.

Harrington, perhaps more than anyone, knew what playing host to the Ryder Cup meant to Ireland. One of his sponsors was Fáilte Ireland, the Irish Tourism Board, and part of the player's remit was to entice golfing tourists to Ireland, which in 2005 won the International Destination of the Year from the International Golf Tour Operators Association.

It was a sell close to Harrington's heart, simply because he firmly believes in the product.

If anything, Harrington felt part of his problem throughout 2006 would be in separating the Ryder Cup hype from the week-in, week-out demands of actual tournament play.

Speaking to him at the time, he said: 'I can't allow myself to get involved in all the hype, that excitement of the Ryder Cup. As players, we'd never perform and make the team if we got involved in the hype. We have to play our own individual tournaments, one by one, and not get caught up in the hype. You have to worry about yourself and what you are doing, and not to worry about the bigger picture. But it will be interesting to see how I cope during the season, to see how I can deflect some of the attention away from myself so that I am not getting too hyped up about the Ryder Cup when I am trying to compete in other events.'

Ask Harrington about the attractions of an Irish golfing vacation for overseas visitors, and his answer is unequivocal.

'The people. That's the number one attraction,' he said. 'We've obviously got fantastic golf courses. We've great places to stay. We've great culture. We've great entertainment. But the best thing about Ireland is its people, the relaxed atmosphere. The people enjoy themselves. They're easy going, friendly, helpful. It is what will make the Ryder Cup in Ireland so special.

'I think people coming to Ireland from the United States will find it amazing that the man in the street, not just golf enthusiasts, will be talking about the Ryder Cup and they'll be truly interested in it. Everyone will be talking about it: housewives, working men, everyone. The whole country will be into it, which will be crazy. You won't be able to get away from it.'

On that January afternoon, Harrington, for one, believed Europe would have their hands full if a third successive Ryder Cup victory over the United States was to be claimed in his homeland.

'To be honest, we couldn't have picked a better venue for the Americans. I mean, we've got a US style golf course designed by Arnold Palmer. They are staying on site in a magnificent hotel where many of them have stayed before. If we were going to pick a venue to negate home advantage, that's where you would pick it; and if you were going to pick a country to negate home advantage, Ireland would be it too.

'We Irish have quite an affinity with the US. A lot of the Americans travelling over here will have Irish backgrounds. I think a lot of the Irish supporters will support the European team strongly but will be very encouraging and respectful of the US team. Many Irish golf fans are particular fans of the American players, of Tiger and Phil, and many others. They would all get a good welcome. I would see the crowd as being very loud, very supportive, and very fair.

'We'd have a better chance of winning this if we had lost the last Ryder Cup. The fact that we won the last two gives the Americans the momentum to come out here and play good golf, to play strong.

'I think all the things Europe used in the past will be going for the Americans this time. I don't know why the Americans haven't performed in the last two. I think Europe has played great ... but we have certainly overachieved in the matches. When you have all our players overachieving, I suppose it is not good enough to have the Americans turning up with 12 players and six playing well and six playing average.

'The K Club is the ideal Ryder Cup venue ... we have spectacular, world class golf courses all over Ireland, but they are golf courses rather than venues in that you need to have all the infrastructure that goes with a golf course to play host to the Ryder Cup. The K Club is ideal. The golf course is world class, the hotel is world class. It always has been a matchplay style golf course and it is going to really blossom for the Ryder Cup,' he added.

His talk was of someone who fully expected to be part of the European team. This was only January, a time when he was preparing for a new campaign after a winter's mix of rest and ongoing work on his swing, so he was entitled to be optimistic. In the end, the wait to secure his place would mathematically go all the way to the last qualifying event, the BMW International in Munich.

TWO

Bullets, Birdies and a Tale of Two Drivers

April 2006, Augusta, Georgia.

TOM LEHMAN HAD A NUMBER of things on his mind as he drove along the Bobby Jones Expressway on the Tuesday night before the Masters Tournament at Augusta National Golf Club. Sure, he was the captain of the United States team for the Ryder Cup, but his early season form was such that there was actually a good chance of playing his way onto the team. Would he play? Could he be a non-playing captain? Might he give up the captaincy?

On this night in April, Lehman was driving down an inside lane on a road named after one of America's legendary golfers, a man who was feted to two tickertape parades in New York and who was the inspiration for creating Augusta National Golf Club. Lehman had earlier spent the day playing a practice round at the famed course and, now, as the sun was setting, he was heading to the airport at Bush Field to pick up his wife, Melissa, his children, and some family friends.

As Lehman prepared to take an exit off the expressway, he thought he heard a sound similar to a firecracker. For an instant, it occurred to Lehman that someone had shot at him; but he dismissed the notion. After all, no windows were broken and the tyres were still intact. He continued undeterred to the airport in his car, alone with his thoughts.

It was only when Lehman got to the airport that the reality of what had happened was brought home. Out of curiosity, he decided to check out his luxury SUV, and that's when he discovered a bullet had pierced a backseat door and had lodged in the seat behind. It seemed that Lehman had been the innocent victim of a random drive-by shooting.

'It was a very, very surreal experience,' said Lehman. 'You don't have guys shooting at you very often.'

Lehman wasn't the only driver that night to experience such an incident. When he made his discovery, he informed police of what had happened. He didn't want anyone else to go through the same experience. It was too late. The police had just received a separate report of another drive-by shooting on the Bobby Jones Expressway. Like Lehman, thankfully, nobody had been injured and an arrest had been made. Once the suspect was in custody, investigators linked the two crimes together, finding weapons and spent casings.

Lehman was grateful the shooting occurred on the way to the airport—and not after he picked up his family. His 10-year-old son, Thomas, could have been sitting in the seat where the bullet ended up.

'We were all joking around and looking at the car, but Thomas was very upset,' said Lehman's wife, Melissa. 'He kept asking, "Who did that? Who did that?" He really loves his dad.'

The shooting incident in Augusta was a distraction, albeit an unwelcome one, for Lehman. He had come to the Masters answering as many questions about his own game as about others who were likely to qualify for the United States team for the Ryder Cup match at The K Club. The American qualifying system was changed after the record-sized defeat to Europe in the 2004 match at Oakland Hills, outside Detroit, to give greater weight to in-form players. So it was that top-10 finishes by American players in tournaments in the second of the two-year qualifying process earned higher points for players. Lehman's tied-seventh finishes in the AT&T Pebble Beach Pro-Am and the Nissan Open in Los Angeles, and a fourth place finish in the WGC-Accenture Match Play Championship in San Diego in February of 2006, had propelled him into contention for a place on his own team.

Lehman, though, was to miss the cut at Augusta National, and, as the summer turned to autumn, calls for his inclusion in the United States team turned from a roar into a whisper. It was only when he finished tied-second in the International tournament in Denver, Colorado, the penultimate counting event in U.S. qualifying, that his name was again strongly mentioned as a possible team member. A win in the International would have automatically secured his place. Such is the thin line between automatic qualifying, and not.

Back in April, the American team was shaping up to be a contrasting one, made up of experience and inexperience. Tiger Woods and Phil Mickelson, the two biggest names in world golf, had already been guaranteed their places, but other so-called lesser lights, among them Vaughn Taylor, who had grown up on the wrong side of the tracks in Augusta, had emerged as possible players for the match in Ireland.

The Masters tournament is the first of the season's majors, but it has the smallest field of any of the four major championships, the others being the US Open, the Open Championship and the US PGA. Those who play in Augusta National do so at the invitation of the Masters Committee and, although the leading 50 players in the world rankings are assured of an invite, there are also places reserved for the winners of the leading US Amateur Championship and the British Amateur Championship. This link with tradition has to do with the desires of Bobby Jones, the man who found an old orchard in Georgia and thought it prime real estate for a golf course. He had remained an amateur throughout his career, but competed successfully against professional players.

The course at Augusta National Golf Club, an exclusive club that to this day refuses to accept women members, is positioned on Washington Road. Apart from the golf club, which is hidden behind a line of magnolia trees and has an entrance that is guarded by security throughout the year, Washington Road is a tribute to modern day America. It boasts a series of low grade motels, fast food restaurants, a Hooters bar and a number of small shopping malls. There are also a number of churches in close proximity and, conversely, if you venture into downtown Augusta, a seedier side to the city can be viewed, with a number of strip joints on the main thoroughfare.

For many golfers the world over, Augusta National is a golfing haven. For the Masters tournament each year, it is always in pristine condition; but it has changed considerably in more recent years in an effort perceived as 'tiger-proofing' the course to combat the game's long hitters.

Since Woods burst onto the professional scene, winning the first of his four Masters green jackets in 1997, Augusta National undertook some dramatic changes to the course. In the year since Woods won his fourth Masters title in 2005, course architect Tom Fazio was brought in to make further adjustments, lengthening the course by 155 metres. As Augusta National Chairman Hootie Johnson put it:

'Since the first Masters in 1934, this golf course has evolved and that process continues … as in the past, our objective is to maintain the integrity and shot values of the golf course as envisioned by Bobby Jones and Alister Mackenzie. Players' scores are not a factor. We will keep the golf course current with the times.'

That April, not everyone was happy with what had occurred. Two greats of the game, Jack Nicklaus and Arnold Palmer, who no longer compete in the tournament, were highly critical of the alterations.

'Whether they've gone overboard I'm not sure,' was the comment of Nicklaus, who observed, 'I love the place, love everything that happens there … (but) it's changed dramatically from the course I played 50 years ago.'

Change is nothing new, however. Ironically, given Nicklaus' reservations about the latest changes, there were changes in the '60s too, to counteract the perceived big-hitting of some players, Nicklaus especially. On that occasion, additional fairway bunkering was constructed. But, compared with the changes since 1999, they were minor, nip'n'tuck surgery.

The facelifts since then have been more severe, and the latest modification the most severe of all. Since Woods had beaten Chris DiMarco in a play-off in the 2005 tournament, four Par 4s (the first, seventh, 11th and 17th), the Par 3 fourth and the Par 5 15th had all been lengthened; and toughened in other ways, by the planting of additional trees and increasing the size of some fairway bunkers.

Mickelson and Woods once again came in as favourites. But Woods did so knowing that his father, Earl, was losing his long fight against cancer and that this would most probably be the last major championship he would see his son play in.

For Mickelson, there were no such ulterior concerns. He came into the Masters on the back of a record-breaking win in the previous week's BellSouth Classic at the TPC at Sugarloaf in Duluth, outside Atlanta, where he had experimented for the Masters by playing with two drivers. Much to the amazement of most observers, Mickelson insisted he was seriously contemplating using two drivers in the actual Masters.

Once, at the peak of his powers, Colin Montgomerie had made the observation:

'You need a driver to win the US Open, and a putter to win the US Masters.'

Such an observation only seemed to confirm how much things had changed so quickly in modern golf, as exemplified by Mickelson's decision to include two drivers in his bag in the quest for a second green jacket in three years.

Where once it was possible to drive the ball onto broad fairways at Augusta National, the metamorphosis in the course's set-up—with additional trees, longer holes, narrower landing areas, and rough, meant that the driver was an increasingly important weapon in a golfer's armoury.

Mickelson, recognising this and seeking to utilise one of his strong points, decided to put that second driver into his bag at the expense of a sand wedge. Mickelson's drivers had different shaft lengths: one of 44 inches and one of 46. One was designed to extenuate drawing the ball, the other to help in fading it.

'Our new slogan at Callaway is the only thing better than an FT3 driver is two FT3 drivers,' was the proclamation from a confident Mickelson ahead of the tournament, adding: 'I decided there were too many shots off the tee where I needed different distances and these drivers are different distances. All of the right-to-left holes, I didn't have to hit it very hard; and all of the left-to-right holes, I had to hit it pretty far. I have a driver I hit a long ways that draws, and I have a driver that fades and stays in play.'

.   .   .   .

If Mickelson wanted the perfect test run for his reasoning, it came at the BellSouth where he hit 64 of 72 greens in regulation and finished with a 65 for a winning total of 28-under 280. José María Olazábal, showing fine early season form in his quest to automatically make a return to the European Ryder Cup team for the first time since 1999, and Zach Johnson, another of those bidding to make a debut appearance on the United States team, had finished tied-second, 13 shots behind.

Speaking about the two drivers concept at the time, Mickelson was philosophical about the advantage it gave him. 'The way the internal weighting of the club [is], one draws it and takes the left side out of play; and one fades it, and takes the right side out of play. It's great because I only have to play with half the trouble.'

His decision to replace a sand wedge with a driver caused some raised eyebrows, but not an undue amount of surprise.

'I can see his decision of not playing a sand wedge and I can see his decision of two drivers,' said Harrington, who used a longer 47 inch shaft on his driver in the final round of the BellSouth with the intention of using it in Augusta.

'If I was allowed 15 clubs this week, the decision would be between an extra lob wedge and a second driver. Technically it is a driver plus a strong three-wood, so that the second three-wood is your driver. I can see where he is coming from.'

Michael Campbell, the 2005 US Open champion, could also see the logic. 'I can understand where Phil is coming from because, as they lengthen courses like Augusta, the emphasis is more on driving accuracy.'

As he stood outside the elegant clubhouse, Paul McGinley smiled at the news of Mickelson's ingenuity.

'Phil thinks outside the box, that's one thing you have got to give him credit for. He is a leader, not a follower. I'm a fan of Mickelson in general, I think he is good for the game. I mean, here's me making a big debate as to whether to put in the new Taylormade ball, which is absolutely a world class golf ball and one that I'll be using very quickly, and he is putting in two drivers and taking out a sand wedge. It is a pretty ballsy decision to make.'

• • • •

THE GOLFING GODS DON'T DEAL in sentiment. Once upon a time, James Joyce, not an avid golfer, was to remark: 'Sentimentality is an unearned emotion.'

And, on the final day of the US Masters tournament, the author's point was proven as, one by one, fate ignored the just claims of a handful of golfers to a green jacket and instead bestowed its blessings on Mickelson, fast becoming a favoured son.

One by one they fell away, those who thought this would be their time: Fred Couples, seeking to become the oldest Masters winner of them all; Rocco Mediate, whose career had been blighted by serious back injury; Darren Clarke, whose wife, Heather, was battling secondary cancer; and Woods, whose father was on his deathbed.

And while the whims of the course inflicted its punishment on others, Mickelson—runaway winner in the BellSouth Classic the previous week—kept his focus to secure his third major title. A final round 69 for seven-under-par 280 gave 'Lefty' a second successive major, following his US PGA win at Baltusrol, New Jersey, the previous August, and his second Masters title in three years.

That Sunday in Georgia was a beautiful day, a stark contrast to the rain and thunderstorms that hit the course on the Saturday, when the third round was left incomplete after a four hour-plus weather delay. The final round leader board at times was as congested as Washington Road. That is, until Mickelson escaped his pursuers to leave them all in his wake.

In the end, Mickelson—giving a masterful performance, bogey free until the last hole—had two strokes to spare over runner-up Tim Clark, who holed out of a greenside bunker for a finishing birdie on his 72nd hole. The South African finished with a 69 for 283, for a career-best second-place finish in a major.

The biggest charge of the final round came from Spain's José María Olazábal. The Masters champion of 1994 and 1999—

almost reverential about this course that has played such a part in his career—eagled the 15th hole in a 66, the best round of the tournament, for four-under 284.

'I feel at peace with myself out there. I looked at the leader board, saw the guys weren't making a charge and thought, okay, see how you play and you might have a chance. I was enjoying myself.'

Olazábal finished tied-third in a five-man group with Woods, who birdied four of his last six holes, Couples, Chad Campbell and Retief Goosen.

'I putted atrociously,' Woods was to lament afterwards, of his futile bid to catch Mickelson. 'Tee-to-green, it's the best I've hit it in years but that's as bad as I've putted. I'll probably go and snap this putter into eight pieces.'

What had started as a day of huge anticipation for the two Irish players in the field, Clarke and Harrington, finished with disappointment. From being in serious contention, the two slipped away. Clarke had actually started his final round with a 25-footer for a birdie to get within a stroke of 54-holes leader Mickelson. It was as good as it got, though.

The greens were so slick that at times it was a challenge for players to simply keep the ball on the putting surface, as evidenced by Harrington's plight on the ninth. The Dubliner's putt from 30 feet above the hole refused to stop until it found the bottom of the hill some 25 yards in front of the green. Back-to-back bogeys for Clarke on the fifth and sixth holes of his final round halted his momentum. Clarke eventually finished with a 77 for 291, three-over, leaving him in tied-22nd.

Clarke could do nothing but shake his head. 'Just nothing happened, nothing at all. Everything that had a chance of going in stayed out. It was just one of those days.'

The Ulsterman wasn't the only one to see his dreams unrealised. Mediate, for one, had stayed in the thick of things until walking to the 11th tee for the last time. By the time he walked off the green of the tournament's hardest hole some 505 yards later, Mediate— who had put three balls in the creek, twice on his approach and again after splashing out from a greenside bunker—was signing for a sextuplet ten and his quest was well and truly over.

It was a day when many dreams were shattered. When Harrington reached the course at 6.15am to start the warm-up routine for his incomplete third round, it was with great expectations. His first putt of the morning would be a six-footer for a birdie that would take him to within a stroke of the lead. What ensued would be a microcosm of a terrible old day at the office, as the Dubliner not only missed his birdie putt, but saw it spin 12-feet by the hole and result in a three putt. It would be his first of three three-putts in a round that also featured two double-bogeys, at the 13th and 15th.

It was a dispiriting morning's performance; and when Harrington started his final round with missed putts at the first two holes from eight feet, the writing was very much on the wall.

'I became very frustrated. I badly needed a fast start if I was to make up ground … I wouldn't say there was a mental strain, I would say it was down to tiredness.'

. . . .

IN THE GATHERING GLOOM, THE age-old ceremony was enacted. As always happens on the Sunday evening of the Masters, the previous year's champion slips a green jacket onto the shoulders of his successor. In 2005, Woods was the recipient. This time, he was the giver as he slipped the precious jacket that remains within the confines of Augusta National on to Mickelson.

Mickelson, an All-American with a winning smile, was a changed man. He had gone from a player who couldn't win a major for love nor money to a player stockpiling the game's most prestigious prizes faster than anyone else. And, in the cosy confines of the Butler Cabin on Sunday evening, as Woods—still the world's number one—traded green jackets with Mickelson, one couldn't help but feel that finally a modern-day rivalry to match the days of Jack and Arnie had truly materialised.

This is how it used to be with the old Mickelson: in his first 42 appearances in major championships, he failed to win even one. Not one. And this was how it was with the new Mickelson: his second US Masters victory was his third major title win in nine starts, and the second in a row after his success in the previous August's US PGA championship. Mickelson had now won a major for each of the last three seasons, a sequence started with his 2004 Masters win.

'Three-for-nine sounds better, huh?' was his response, when reminded of the 0-for-42 statistic.

Mickelson's transformation into a winning machine was not a solo effort, and the evolution from nearly-man to a winner could be traced back to the painstaking work he undertook with his coaches, with swing guru Rick Smith and short game expert Dave Pelz, prior to the breakthrough major win at Augusta National in 2004.

'There's no doubt he's changed,' said Fred Couples. 'He's an incredible player. He's got more talent than maybe anyone out there in his hands and in his game.'

Harnessing that talent was always Mickelson's problem. But prior to the 2004 Masters, the American changed his preparations, visiting Augusta National in the weeks beforehand and working on different shots. This time round, he showed an ability to 'think outside the box,' as McGinley put it, by having those two drivers in his bag for the extra length of the course.

In his champion's press conference in the permanent structure that houses the world's golfing press each April, Mickelson was reminded of the fact that Nicklaus and Palmer traded the green jacket back and forth between 1962 and 1966 and that, now, himself and Woods have done it three years in a row.

'Well, you know, I don't really want to trade next year ... but I certainly enjoyed having the jacket put on me rather than putting it on someone else. I don't know if it is good for the game or not, but I love the chance to compete against guys like Tiger, guys like Retief [Goosen] and Ernie [Els] and Vijay [Singh] and Fred [Couples] who are playing so well. It gives me an incredible feeling of accomplishment to be able to come out on top.'

Of his growing collection of major titles and the fact that the win sets in motion thoughts of a Grand Slam, Mickelson responded:

'I don't really think of that. As much as I want to be part of the history of this tournament and a part of the history of the great game of golf, it's not something I dwell on. I really enjoy the challenges that each major presents ... I don't think about leaving a legacy. I just try to play well and compete and hopefully win as many as I can. It's nice that I've started because two years ago I wasn't.'

Mickelson also became the first player since Woods in 2002 to win back-to-back majors, and this latest success has naturally led to thoughts of him accomplishing the so-called 'Tiger Slam' of winning four successive majors; and, perhaps, even the elusive Grand Slam, of all four majors in the one season. The next part of that equation would be the US Open in June at Winged Foot, a championship Mickelson was to remember for all the wrong reasons.

THREE

Troubled Times

THERE WAS AN OBVIOUS SADNESS about Tiger Woods as he left Augusta National in April, and not entirely because he had failed to win. Nobody wants to win as badly as Woods, but he is a good loser. He accepts defeat manfully. The sadness had to do with the knowledge that his father, Earl, who had been too ill to attend the Masters tournament, would never see him win another major championship.

On Sunday, 9 April, as the car containing Woods, who had not long before placed the green jacket on the shoulders of Phil Mickelson, drove down Magnolia Lane and out onto Washington Road, the world's number one golfer knew he would not play competitive golf again for quite some time.

The immediate future, and who was to know how long after, would be a time to spend with his father, and then to grieve.

On 3 May 2006, Earl Woods, who was the driving force behind the greatest golfer of the modern age, died at home in Cypress, California. He was 74. Tiger would not play again until the US Open championship at Winged Foot, New York, in June, where he would miss the cut in a major for the first time in his professional career.

Woods let the world know of his grief in a personal message on his website soon after his father passed away:

'My dad was my best friend and greatest role model, and I will miss him deeply. I'm overwhelmed when I think of all of the great things he accomplished in his life. He was an amazing dad, coach, mentor, soldier, husband and friend. I wouldn't be where I am today without him, and I'm honoured to continue his legacy of sharing and caring.'

Earl Woods was a habitual smoker, who had heart bypass surgery in 1986. He was diagnosed with prostate cancer in 1998, and as part of his treatment was given radiation therapy. But the cancer returned in 2004 and spread throughout his body. Throughout all of his treatment over this period of time, he never failed to make it to Augusta National for the Masters tournament.

His son had made his debut in the tournament as an amateur in 1995 and, as a 21-year-old professional, won his first green jacket in 1997. One of the enduring memories of recent Masters tournaments was the wholehearted embrace that father and son shared after that win in 1997.

When Eldrick 'Tiger' Woods was born on 30 December, 1975, Earl Woods, who served two tour of duties in Vietnam in the United States Special Forces, where he rose to the rank of Lieutenant Colonel, kept a promise he had made to a friend. He called his son Tiger.

Nguyen Phong of the South Vietnamese Army had been nicknamed 'Tiger' by Earl because of his courage and bravery. 'I knew Tiger was special the day he was born,' Earl was to remark of his son. He introduced Tiger to golf by setting up a makeshift practice range in his garage, with a mat and net, swinging a club as his son watched in a high chair. Tiger appeared on the Mike Douglas Show on network television in the United States at two years of age and even played exhibitions with Sam Snead and Jack Nicklaus.

Earl Woods gave Tiger his love of golf. In the foreword to his father's book, Woods was to write: 'In retrospect, golf for me was an apparent attempt to emulate the person I looked up to more than anyone: my father. He was instrumental in helping me develop the drive to achieve, but his role—as well as my mother's—was one of support and guidance, not interference.'

Of his son, Earl Woods was to remark, 'He's the bridge between the East and the West … there is no limit because he has the guidance. I don't know yet exactly what form this will take. But he is the Chosen One. He'll have the power to impact nations. Not people. Nations. The world is just getting a taste of his power.'

. . . .

Maynooth, Ireland. May 2006.

So MUCH FOR THE IRISH summer. The Nissan Irish Open at Carton House, a walled demesne just outside Maynooth in Co. Kildare, had been dogged by brutal weather. If it wasn't high winds, it was torrential, unrelenting rain. The tournament, one of the most prized titles on the PGA European Tour, had attracted a very strong field but the tough conditions left many players empathising with drowned rats and wondering what on earth they had done to deserve such punishment. 'The past week has been like working in the engine room of the Titanic,' resort superintendent John Plummer was to remark of the run of adverse weather conditions.

One of those who ignored the elements and kept his head down was Darren Clarke. He, more than anyone, knew that golf was not a matter of life and death. All he had to do was think of the battle his wife, Heather, was fighting with cancer, to know that he was one of the fortunate ones. These days, golf, for Clarke, was a refuge from life's complexities. His outings on tour in 2006 were limited, but he was determined to make the most of them and, in yet a further measure of his innate golfing ability, it was all the more remarkable that time after time Clarke found himself in contention going into the business end of a tournament.

Such was the case at Carton House, a fine golfing resort developed by the Mallaghan family not too far removed from The K Club. Once upon a time, Carton House had been home to the Earl of Kildare and through the years had hosted royalty and celebrities, among them Queen Victoria, Prince Rainier and Grace Kelly. The estate had also provided the backdrop to many television and film productions, including Stanley Kubrick's *Barry Lyndon*.

On the Saturday afternoon of the Irish Open, a different kind of television viewing acted as a distraction to Clarke as he prepared to putt out on the 18th green. The previous day, after finishing his third round, Clarke had described his golf as 'horrific' and claimed that he 'couldn't be bothered any more.' Yet, here he was completing his third round on the Montgomerie Course with a chance to equal the course record 65 set by his friend Thomas Bjørn the previous day, when Clarke couldn't resist taking a glance at the giant screen which had been erected in the public village on the other side of the river.

The screen was showing the Heineken Cup rugby final between Munster and Biarritz, and Clarke, who had played rugby in his youth in Dungannon, momentarily lost concentration as he strained his eyes to see how the match was developing.

'I just went blank,' he was to explain later, referring to how his birdie putt from little more than 18 inches lipped out on the last hole. Instead of signing for a 66, Clarke put his signature to a 67 in the recorder's hut stationed behind the 18th green. It left him a stroke behind 54-holes leader Bjørn, and in with a chance to become the first Irishman to win the Irish Open since John O'Leary accomplished the feat in 1982.

Bjørn, like Clarke, had included making Europe's Ryder Cup team as one of his season's goals. At Oakland Hills, outside Detroit, in 2004, the Dane had been reduced to a so-called 'lieutenant' as part of captain Bernhard Langer's back-room team. His had been a forceful presence in the team locker-room but Bjørn wanted badly to be a playing part of the team for the match at The K Club.

Given his comments after Ian Woosnam's 'wild card' selections come August, the words that Bjørn uttered at Carton House at that time would come back to haunt him.

'If I want to be on the team, I think I might have to play my way in. Woosie's in a situation where he is going to need his two wild cards. In saying that, it is not life-or-death for me, but I would like to be there for the only reason that I know I am playing the right sort of golf.'

At that time, it must be said, destiny was in Bjørn's own hands. Unlike Clarke, who had missed a tiny putt on the 18th, a Par 5 that runs along the River Rye, Bjørn had finished his third round by holing a 40-foot eagle putt. It more than made up for the eight he had incurred on the same hole in his opening round just a day earlier. Bjørn's first round didn't finish until the Friday, due to a six-hour suspension in play on the Thursday because of high winds, but that triple-bogey eight on the way to a first round 78 included the ignominy of a fresh air shot. Before his second round, Bjørn had a quick talk with his psychologist, the Belgian Jos Vanstiphout, and proceeded to shoot 12 shots better, signing for a 66. At the end of the third round, he was leading the tournament.

Bjørn, as leader, was in fine fettle on the Saturday evening, yet also aware that his good friend Clarke was continuing to produce remarkably good golf in what were extremely trying personal circumstances.

'My friendship with Darren goes way beyond golf,' said Bjørn. 'We take a big interest in what goes on in our personal lives, and it is always nice to see him play well. The final round is a working day for both of us, but he needs good things to happen to him at the moment and he needs it on the golf course.'

Sunday, 21 May was a miserable day. The start time for the final round of the Irish Open was brought forward in an attempt to complete the golf tournament before a forecast storm hit this piece of prime real estate in Co. Kildare, but even that contingency plan didn't work. The weather closed in before the final round could be completed and the final three-ball of Bjørn, Paul Casey and Anthony Wall had only reached the eighth green when a decision was taken to suspend play.

The tournament organisers had two options. One was to revert to the position after 54 holes, in which case Bjørn would be the winner. The other option was to take the tournament into a fifth day. The fact that the following week's event was the BMW International at The Wentworth Club, outside London, making flight connections and travel plans viable, made it easier to extend the tournament and that was the choice made by Tournament Director David Probyn, who broke the news to competitors in the players' lounge in the late afternoon. The announcement was met with one or two shakes of the head by some players who simply wanted to get away, but the majority of players voiced a sentiment of 'good decision' back to the bearer of the news.

As tournament director Probyn was to observe: 'It's a question of majority over minority,' stressing the point that most players had completed the majority of the final round, and PGA European Tour chief referee Andy McFee went on to explain the preference of finishing all four rounds.

'It goes to the very credibility of your sport, that's absolutely key. Sometimes it would be just plain wrong to go back to the 54 hole mark because so much of the final round has been completed … it's a sensible decision to take, that 72 holes is the benchmark of professional golf and, if you convert the tournament back to 54 holes, that is in the record books forever and a day.'

Clarke, not surprisingly, was one of those eager to continue. He had planned a day's fishing with his father, Godfrey, on the River Test in Surrey for the following day but in the eight holes he had played on this miserable Sunday weather-wise, he had played some beautiful golf and recorded three birdies in managing to claim the undisputed lead. Just minutes before the claxon to suspend play sounded, Clarke, his grip slipping on the wet shaft, had blocked his drive into heavy rough on the ninth hole. 'It was my own fault, I had plenty of towels to dry my clubs and I didn't dry it properly,' he was to remark.

When Clarke returned to his ball at 9.15am on Monday morning to complete his fourth round, he discovered some leprechauns, or other unnamed persons, had been to work overnight. Instead of being surrounded by thick grass as it had been when he'd departed the scene the previous day, the ball was now sitting up nicely without even a tuft of grass to cause interference, and offered the player a seven-iron shot that would comfortably reach the front of the green. The player wasn't happy with his improved lie and called European Tour referee Mikael Eriksson and informed him of the new developments.

Eriksson acknowledged that someone had improved the lie, but informed Clarke that, under the Rules of Golf, he was entitled to play the ball as it now was. Clarke wasn't happy, and explained why.

'All of the ball was there and there wasn't much grass around it. The ruling was to play the ball as it lies. I hadn't broken any rules or done anything wrong ... but I couldn't let myself do it. My conscience wouldn't allow me to do that. I'd have held my head in shame walking all the way up to the green, so I decided to chip it out (to the fairway) and play it as I would have done yesterday (on Sunday).'

Which is what Clarke did, pitching back out on to the fairway instead of going for the green. It was the first shot of his resumed fourth round, but it was not to lead to the victory that the galleries, who had returned on another wet morning, had wished to see.

Unfortunately for Clarke, the win that he so desperately wanted evaded his clutches. As on the Sunday, the Ulsterman showed a great deal of patience in his play. His manager, Chubby Chandler, had sent him a text message before he went out to play, preaching: 'Patience … patience … patience … f***ing patience.'

Before the resumed fourth round, Chandler delivered the same message in person and, for much of the morning, it seemed to have the desired effect. Even when the birdie putts failed to drop, Clarke remained patient. Even when he bogeyed the 16th where he failed to get up-and-down after missing the green with his approach, he stayed patient. Standing on the 18th tee, he was still in a share of the lead (on four-under with Casey in the match behind, but shortly to be joined by Bjørn) and knowing that destiny was in his own hands.

Clarke's drive down the Par 5 18th was a superb one, and left him with a three-wood approach to the green. On playing the fairway wood, though, he 'moved ahead' of the ball, as he was to put it later, which resulted in the ball coming up short of the green. But it didn't seem to be any major error. What happened next, however, proved punishing.

'I tried to play a sand wedge off the back of my stance, to chase it all the way up the green,' explained Clarke. But he caught it heavy, and then compounded the error by three-putting from 40 feet for a finishing bogey.

Harrington, who had come up short in his own bid to win the title, had re-emerged from the recorder's cabin and went to the back of the 18th green to see Clarke's closing efforts and was as disappointed as the galleries who had trudged around the course in the hope of a first Irish winner since 1982. He was to surmise:

'I feel for Darren, of course I do … the whole idea is to get yourself in contention and put yourself out there (to win). But when it doesn't work out, it is not a nice experience. Darren will obviously take confidence in the fact that it is a lot better to have been there (contending) than the 60 or 70 players who all made the cut but who are saying, 'if only'. It's tough because he was there.'

Even Bjørn, the eventual victor, admitted that his thoughts at times had wandered to the possibilities of a Clarke win.

'There's no person in the world I would rather see winning at the moment than Darren ... we have a great relationship and I have the utmost respect for him as a person and all of his family. You know, it's not the easiest of times (for them). I go to bed every night praying for him and his family.'

On that Monday morning, before they had headed out in pursuit of the Irish Open title, Bjørn had offered Clarke a lift on his plane home to London. It was a sign of their friendship. Win or lose, they would travel on to Wentworth together. When word reached Bjørn of the stance that Clarke had taken on discovering his ball in an improved lie on his return to the course to complete his fourth round, it very nearly brought tears to the great Dane's eyes, and he re-stated his admiration for his friend.

'Darren's as good a sportsman as they come. He puts a lot of pride in putting the game above everything else and what he did on the ninth just shows his character and his belief in the game. The game of golf is much, much bigger than any person. We play under rules and we have to play by those rules ourselves ... we have to set an example to amateur golfers around the world about how this game is played and Darren is a great example of how a professional sportsman should treat the sport.'

· · · ·

Virginia Water, Surrey, England. May 2006.

EVERY YEAR, ON THE EVE of the BMW Championship at the Wentworth Club, set in the heart of the Surrey stockbroker belt, the PGA European Tour's annual dinner is staged. On this night,

Michael Campbell, the New Zealander who won the 2005 US Open championship at Pinehurst, North Carolina, was being feted. He wasn't the only one to notice the array of wedges and fairway woods adorning the walls in the entrance lobby and hallway leading to the banquet.

The clubs, donated by winners of the various championships held on the West Course, are testimony to the rich history of Wentworth, and its place in the game of golf. There's a natural tendency for anyone walking down the hallway to take a look at the little brass plaques placed under each club. A driver donated by Ernie Els. A wedge donated by Seve Ballesteros. The list is a roll of honour of the great and the good in professional golf.

Wentworth has only once played host to the Ryder Cup, in 1953, but, in many ways, it is the birthplace of the competition. The Ryder Cup grew out of an informal match between a team of professionals from the United States and Britain that was played in 1926 at Wentworth, a match when Bobby Jones shot an immaculate round of 66 with 33 shots and 33 putts, taking 33 shots going out and 33 shots coming in.

'We should do this again,' is the comment attributed to the seed merchant Samuel Ryder, who was buying drinks at the bar after that informal match, and so was born the Ryder Cup.

David Howell had not played the previous week's Nissan Irish Open, but he arrived at the BMW Championship, an event previously called the Volvo PGA and the flagship tournament of the PGA European Tour, virtually certain of his place on Woosnam's team for the defence of the Ryder Cup at The K Club. Howell had made his debut on the team at Oakland Hills in 2004 and, while acquitting himself well there, had grown into one of the strong men of European golf in the interim. Come September, the expectation was that he would be one of those players that Woosie would lean on.

Among those players that Howell had impressed was Tiger Woods. The pair had gone toe-to-toe in the HSBC Champions tournament at Sheshan International Golf Club in Shanghai, the previous November, and Howell had stayed so calm under pressure that Woods subsequently referred to him simply as 'Cool Dude'. The appendage stuck. Others saw it as a rather appropriate moniker for the laid-back Englishman with an assassin's ruthlessness.

As he walked to the first tee in front of the Wentworth Club shortly before 2pm on the Sunday for the final round, Howell only had to look to the giant leader board positioned to the left of the first fairway to know this BMW Championship was his to lose rather than for others to win.

So, on a day bereft of any inclement weather, but with placing still in operation on fairways sodden by the heavy rain of the previous days, Howell proved to be the true king of the fairways. With three birdies in his opening five holes, Howell ensured that everyone else was playing for second best. He could even afford to finish with six successive pars, including failing to birdie either of the Par 5s at the 17th and 18th holes, to establish the biggest winning margin seen on tour in 2006, beating the four shots of Francesco Molinari at the Italian Open.

In claiming his second title of the season, having previously fended off Woods down the stretch of the HSBC in Shanghai, the winning cheque for €708,330 reaffirmed his status at the top of the European Tour money list and moved him to top of the European Ryder Cup points list. This was as impressive a performance as any in the long history of the PGA, the tour's flagship tournament.

'This win is as big as it comes on the European Tour. I'm absolutely delighted. It's not something I've particularly dreamed of, [because] I guess I never really think great things are going to happen to me. I'm overwhelmed,' Howell was to remark after a closing round 69 for 271, 17-under. Howell eventually finished five shots clear of Simon Khan, with Miguel Angel Jimenez a stroke further back in third.

'Once I played 17 I knew I had it. I mean, you know someone can conceivably finish 3-3 on those last two holes. If you make seven on 17, all of a sudden things are different. That's the way you've got to think … so, once I got to the 17th green, I was able to relax. It was the ideal scenario, and that's exactly what you dream of so that you can enjoy the walk down the last hole.'

For the 30-year-old follower of Swindon Town Football Club, the win—and the manner of it—put him onto a new level. Still, there is never any bigheadedness associated with Howell, and he was quick to point out that his feet were staying firmly on the ground.

'I don't see myself as the best player in Europe. I see myself as one of a bunch, but I'm not intimidated by anyone. I play with Darren Clarke every week at Queenwood and he takes £100 off me.'

With his place on Woosnam's team for the Ryder Cup, Howell was left to ponder new goals.

'One of my goals this year is to win the Order of Merit. I've given myself a great chance of that now and that's something I never really dreamed of. Two or three years ago the guys winning the Order of Merit titles seemed to be in different stratospheres than where I was. I guess I've worked my way somewhere close.'

FOUR

Grotesque. Unbelievable. Bizarre. Unprecedented.

Mamaroneck, New York. June 2006.

GOLFER; GOLF COURSE ARCHITECT; AVIATOR; Astute businessman. Arnold Palmer has an aura around him that only the special ones emit. On a June evening at Winged Foot Golf Club in the fashionable neighbourhood of Mamaroneck, just north of Yonkers, in New York State, the great man, the designer of the Palmer Course at The K Club, was running fashionably late.

The first sign of his imminent arrival was a scattering of golf fans, young and old, some 50 yards away. Autograph hunters, clutching notebooks and replica flags, broke like greyhounds from a trap to find their prey and, sure enough, Palmer, dressed immaculately in blazer, with not a hair out of place, appeared—with a small entourage in tow—and signed the different items politely pushed towards him.

'I thought it was hard to win the US Open. Getting in here [to Winged Foot, venue for the 2006 US Open] was harder,' quipped Palmer. It seems his appointed Colombian limousine driver wasn't entirely *au fait* with the roads network around Mamaroneck and the journey, it transpires, had been every bit as taxing as negotiating a route through a giant maze, only without the fun.

Inside, in an elegantly furnished conference room, Palmer relaxed. Born on 10 September, 1929 in Latrobe, Pennsylvania, Arnold Daniel Palmer has an energy that remains as strong as the period from 1958, when he won his first of four US Masters titles, to the mid-1960s, a time when he dominated the game. In a three year period from 1960 to 1963, he accumulated no fewer than 29 professional titles around the globe and was to be named 'Athlete of the Decade' in the United States.

These days, instead of pursuing titles on the world's fairways, Palmer has a myriad of business commitments that keep his mind busy and his body on the go: he heads Arnold Palmer Enterprises, and has been involved in aviation and car service firms for many years; he is president and sole owner (since 1971) of Latrobe Country Club, and president and principal owner of the Bay Hill Club and Lodge in Orlando, Florida, which he and a group of associates acquired in 1970. In 1999, Palmer and a group of investors purchased the famed Pebble Beach golf complex on the California coast.

It's not just on golf that Palmer has left his mark. A skilled aviator, he is known to fly to many business engagements in his own Cessna Citation X jet. Back in 1976, Palmer was one of a team of four that set a new international record, flying around the world from Denver to Denver in 57 hours, 25 minutes and 42 seconds.

Life is a tad more sedentary now, but, by the template of a normal individual, still extremely busy. Palmer currently has some 25 projects on the go, from places as diverse as China and Panama to France and Indonesia.

'I am doing something I love and what I want to do, and that is to design golf courses,' he said. 'It would never do for me to stop working. I have to continue to be active. I suppose if I stopped being active, I wouldn't last very long.'

He is aware of the criticisms levelled at the Palmer Course. 'It is one of my top golf courses ever. It really has got some great golf holes' he said in his defence. In advance of the match, his critics claimed that it is too American and that a body of opinion exists that the Ryder Cup should have been played on a links.

Palmer responded: 'What can I say? Michael Smurfit is one of the greatest guys I've ever met. He has contributed to Ireland, and he has contributed to the game of golf. He has built a class act in The K Club and I just hope that everyone understands he has done something which I think is pretty fantastic for Ireland and the whole world.

'When I was doing the golf course, I was trying to give a combination of the Irish touch as well as the American touch. You know, I got a little Irish in me too and I liked the thought that it has got an American touch to it but that it is still very Irish. We built a golf course that I thought was just right.'

So, what would he say to those who believed this course provides the American team, who haven't won the trophy since Brookline in 1999, with a gilt-edged opportunity to reclaim the Ryder Cup?

'The K Club, I hope and feel very strongly, will be a great venue for both teams. It will be one that will require a lot of great shot-making. There are a lot of individual challenges on the holes that will challenge the players from both teams, whether it be the water holes, the Par 5 up the river [the 16th], or the 17th, or the 18th, and the little par 3 [14th]. That will be a nice hole.

'We did not try to do something that was real tricky. We tried to do a golf course for the Ryder Cup, for all golf, for Michael Smurfit, [to make it] a challenge that was enjoyable not just for the Ryder Cup but for all people who play golf there. That was our goal. I think the last three holes as they changed them are going to be fun holes ... there's a chance reward situation. You better know what you are doing and be able to carry it off to get the reward that you want.'

On this particular evening in mid-summer, one aspect of the course set-up for the Ryder Cup didn't meet entirely with Palmer's approval, though. And that was the decision to move the tee forward on the Par 5 16th.

'As long as these guys hit it, I don't think they need to move it forward. They can really whip it in there,' insisted Palmer. 'I like the guy who is standing back there, hits a beautiful drive and now he has another challenge, and that second challenge is to be able to hit it onto the green and it is a risk reward situation. If he pushes it a little bit, he is in the water and if he pulls it … [with] 17 and 18, [it's the] same situation.'

Ah, the 17th. Half Moon. Palmer wasn't aware then that it had well and truly shown its teeth, before a shot had been hit in anger in the Ryder Cup. Bjørn took an 11 there on the Par 4 in the final round of the 2005 Smurfit European Open, at a time when he was leading the tournament. Palmer chuckled at the image.

'Did he really? Those [finishing] holes are all risk reward holes. [On] 17, you must keep it left to have a good shot into the green, but you're risking going into the water.'

Palmer's career has been one of many milestones. From the time as a four-year-old when he got a set of cut-down clubs from his father, Milfred (Deacon) Palmer, and discovered his love affair with the game of golf, Palmer—whose legion of fans came to be known as Arnie's Army— has left an indelible imprint on the sport that he came to love and which became his passion.

In his career, he won seven majors (four Masters, two British Opens and one US Open), a career Grand Slam evading him with his failure to claim a US PGA title, a championship where he finished second three times. His winning partnership with Sam Snead in the Canada Cup (now the World Cup) at Portmarnock in 1960 is credited with instigating the phenomenal growth of golf in Ireland, and he was looking forward to the event.

'I played in the World Cup in Ireland and had a great time, and I think it is wonderful we now have the opportunity to play the Ryder Cup there.'

Long before it was cool to be seen as a global player, Palmer started playing in tournaments around the world. He remembers first playing in the British Open, at St Andrews in 1960, when he finished second, losing out by a stroke to Australian Kel Nagle. He was to win back-to-back titles the following two years. He recalled:

'Many years ago, I went to the British Open and I went for all kinds of reasons, one selfish and personal; for the thrill of playing in an open championship, for the thrill of playing at St Andrews. But my motives were many. One was that I had a mind that was saying, wouldn't it be just wonderful if we could do things like have sport as our main objective to world problems? Couldn't we bring it to the sporting field and have football and baseball and golf where we have sport, where we have guys playing their guts out in the name of sport rather than having them shot at in wars?

'And that was an ambition of mine in 1960. Today, I feel the same way ... I feel to some degree we have succeeded, [but] we need to go a lot further and to carry it even further into the world of sport and make it something that is a major objective in the world.'

. . . .

THIS WAS WHERE TIGER WOODS failed to make the cut in a major for the first time as a professional. Playing in his first event since the US Masters, playing in his first event since the death of his father, Woods had shown his fallibility. He's human after all, and those who had survived into the weekend of the US Open at Winged Foot knew that his absence had opened a door that wasn't normally left ajar.

His absence could inspire others. For those Europeans in the field seeking to copper-fasten a place on Ian Woosnam's team, the US Open, and it's huge purse, offered an extra incentive beyond that no player from Europe had managed to win a major since Paul Lawrie won The Open championship at Carnoustie in 1999. That year was also the last time Europe lost a Ryder Cup, the infamous 'Battle of Brookline' at the Country Club in Massachusetts. Given Europe's success in the Ryder Cup since that major triumph by the Scot, it is all the harder to believe than no-one has followed in his footsteps in any of the season's four major championships in the interim.

For those Americans in the field seeking a place on Tom Lehman's team for The K Club, the US Open, with its extra points available should they claim a top-10 finish at Winged Foot, provided extra incentive too, beyond that of chasing the title. Woods may not have survived into the weekend, but his place on the US team had long been assured. Phil Mickelson, Jim Furyk and Chad Campbell were others that captain Lehman had been able to pencil in as the top-half of his team showed strength, at least as far as the world rankings were concerned.

In truth, thoughts of the Ryder Cup were months in the future for those Europeans and Americans competing at Winged Foot. It was the season's second major that was uppermost in their thoughts, competing on a course designed by Arthur Warren Tillinghast.

Tillinghast was asked in 1922 by the New York Athletic Club (the club's logo was the winged foot of the Roman god Mercury, meant to reflect the Manhattan club's track and field programmes in athletics) to design a golf course on 280 acres of rugged terrain in Mamaroneck, and was given just one set of instructions. Give us a man-sized course, he was told.

Tillinghast set his masterpiece on land that was once the choice deer-hunting ground of the Mohican Indians, immortalised by the author James Fenimore Cooper in *The Last of the Mohicans*. The club, with a discreet entrance that befits an upmarket section of Westchester County, can be found on Fenimore Road, named for the writer who roamed the property.

What the foremost architect of his day did was to give the NYAC two courses, the East and the West, each a strategic golf course but so tough that no less a figure than Jack Nicklaus, when asked about the finishing holes on the West Course during the 1974 US Open, remarked, 'the last 18 are very difficult.' That championship, won by Hale Irwin, was so tough that it became known as the 'Massacre at Winged Foot.'

Competitors who arrived early at Winged Foot for the 2006 US Open found a course that was playing long and tough, due to heavy rain. On the weekend before the major, a notice posted by the club's greens committee outside the pro shop informed early arrivals that, 'With two days before the commencement of US Open week, the board believes that potential damage to putting surfaces, tee boxes and fairway and rough areas is too great. This is damage that cannot be repaired prior to the championship.' Those intending to play were asked not to do so.

The weather didn't affect play once the championship got under way, however. And one of those to put down an early marker was Colin Montgomerie. All through his career, his accuracy off the tee had made the US Open one of the majors that he was most likely to win and, now, in the first round he was in the thick of things. But he was also being suitably modest of his aspirations.

'My God, we've only walked seven miles, we've got 21 miles to walk yet. There's a long way to go. But it would probably mean more to me to win now, at 42, than it would have at 32,' Monty was to remark after the first round.

'I think the expectation levels were lower this year,' Montgomerie explained of a more relaxed approach in majors. 'It won't change me if I win here. It won't change my life, or whatever if I do well this week. But it might have done in the '90s. There was more expectation and pressure on me then than there is now. I can go out and free-wheel if you like and not worry about things the way I used to do.'

The surprise leader at the midway stage was Steve Stricker. The bigger surprise was that of Woods missing a cut in a major for the first time as a professional, after a second successive 76 left the world's number one on 152, 12-over, and ready to sail off in his yacht 'Privacy' a couple of days earlier than he had planned. It was a journey that Woods would have preferred to have delayed, as he looked back on the previous few days.

'I just didn't execute properly. I didn't drive the ball all that well. I didn't hit my irons well. Nor did I have the speed [on the greens] again. So that is not a good combo.' Woods' missed cut ended a streak going back 37 championships.

Not afraid to mince his words, Woods, playing for the first time since the death of his father, was to offer no excuses after his second round.

'I am pissed, and that pretty well sums it up. I thought I was playing well enough to shoot an under par round today and I didn't do that. It's not rust. I just unfortunately didn't put it together at the right time … I just felt that if I kept plodding along I could have turned it around with just one putt or just one shot. I just didn't.'

As things transpired, a player with only an outside interest in the Ryder Cup was to win the US Open. Geoff Ogilvy, an Australian who once played on tour in Europe, emerged as the winner, but only after the strangest and most curious finish to a major championship in many a long year.

In the week of the US Open, a former Irish Prime Minister, Charlie Haughey, had died after a long illness. To many in Ireland, his legacy was that he initiated policies that were to lead to the country's economic boom, the so-called 'Celtic Tiger.' To others, his legacy was that he left behind an acronym; GUBU: Grotesque. Unbelievable. Bizarre. Unprecedented; words he had offered up in a debate in the Irish parliament to explain how a double murderer had been apprehended in the home of the government's Attorney General.

As Haughey might have put it, the concluding stages of the US Open at Winged Foot were complete and utter GUBU. With the title within his grasp, Phil Mickelson, who had won the season's first major at Augusta with a control and calm that spoke of a changed character from the one prone to silly mistakes that characterised his early career, contrived to lose a double bogey on the finishing hole to literally hand the crown to Ogilvy.

We shouldn't have been surprised, either at Ogilvy's ability to keep his nerve; or at Mickelson's ability to revert back to his old wayward self when the pressure was at its greatest. For those crowded around the 18th hole, though, Mickelson's actions left them shell-shocked as his final tee shot hit a tent and, then, his attempted approach from a poor lie ricocheted off a tree.

What it meant was that Mickelson's golfing version of pinball down the last resulted in him finishing with a double-bogey six for a 74, which left him on 286. Ten minutes earlier, Ogilvy had finished with a par on the last, getting up and down after coming up short of the green, for a 72. It put him on 285, five-over, and a shot clear of Mickelson, Montgomerie and Jim Furyk. Padraig Harrington finished alone in fifth place, two behind Ogilvy, and ruing a closing run of three successive bogeys.

Mickelson pushed the self-destruct button on the 18th tee, at which stage he had a one stroke lead, by driving left where his ball hit the roof of the hospitality tenting and rebounded onto trampled grass. His route to the green was blocked by trees, but he attempted to curl his approach and proceeded to hit a branch. He was later to confess, 'I can't believe I did that. I am such an idiot.'

The drama was unscripted, a comic-tragedy played out by some of golf's greatest practitioners.

Mickelson was not the only one to reflect on what might have been at Winged Foot. Montgomerie, a winner of eight money titles on the PGA European Tour, had suffered no end of heartbreak stories in a vain quest to win a major. Time and time again, the golfing gods had rebuked him but, now, in this upmarket part of New York, he was to find a chance for redemption. When he holed a 50-foot birdie putt on the 17th hole, to move to four-over for the championship, it seemed that his time had come.

Appropriately, the 18th hole at Winged Foot is called 'Revelations,' and it was to live up to its name. His drive down the 18th was typical Monty; straight down the middle. It left him with an iron approach to the 18th green, the type of shot he would normally execute in his sleep. But he could not make up his mind on the correct club. With playing partner Vijay Singh in trouble in the trees on the left, Montgomerie was left with too much time to think about his shot. When, eventually, he did play it, it was with the wrong club. From the middle of the fairway, the Scot changed his mind on what club to use, opting for a seven-iron instead of a six. He came up short, in thick rough.

'I caught it heavy,' he later explained. He missed the green and then three-putted for a double bogey six to finish. It was to leave him a shot behind Ogilvy.

Padraig Harrington was another player to suffer the wrath of the 18th, only, in his case, his turmoil had come in Saturday's third round when he suffered a triple bogey seven there. Nevertheless, the Irishman, still unsure of a place in Europe's Ryder Cup team at this juncture of the season, had battled his way into the thick of the hunt in the final round. It was an admirable performance.

This is what Harrington wanted—to be in contention in a major coming down the back nine of a Sunday. On the 640 yards Par 5 12th hole, he unleashed a huge drive to the middle of the fairway from where he drew a beautifully controlled long-iron approach to 15 feet. The eagle putt, though, moved left of the hole at the death and left him with a tap-in birdie (his first of the round) to move to five-over. When he holed a 10-footer for birdie on the 14th, Harrington, at that time, moved into a share of the lead.

Things were to unravel over the finishing stretch. Having gone 15 holes without dropping a shot, the only player in the field to accomplish such a feat, Harrington bogeyed the final three holes to finish alone in fifth place, two shots behind Ogilvy. It really was a case of what might or could have been for the Irishman.

Of his near-miss at Winged Foot, Harrington—whose triple-bogey at the 18th in Saturday's third round came after opting to use a rescue club out of heavy rough—insisted that, even in hindsight, he had no regrets.

'No, I definitely don't have any regrets. No. Absolutely not, no regrets at all about anything. I was pushing to do my best at the end and hopefully make birdies coming in. That's the nature of the game ... it wasn't necessary [to make birdies] but who was to know that at the time?'

Harrington, just like Mickelson and Montgomerie and Furyk could only accept their fate, and acknowledged that Ogilvy's time had come.

'The winner does the things right at the end of the day, but he's only a hair's breadth from being like the other guys. It's about getting into position and hoping the cards fall at the right place at the right time,' said Harrington, who at least had some comfort, as he departed Winged Foot, in knowing that he had finally played his way into an automatic place on Europe's Ryder Cup team. That it was the 10th and last automatic spot, however, left him in no doubt either that that there was still much work to be done before he could expect to make the team by right.

FIVE

Is There a Doctor in the House?

Co. Kildare, Ireland. July 2006.

THE MAN IN THE OPEN neck check shirt and faded jeans who stood amidst the crowd outside the John Hume Building at the National University of Ireland, Maynooth, was out of place with those around him. He was a professor in nuclear physics, originally from Ukraine but working in California, and for some reason he had found himself in the middle of the throng outside the new lecture auditorium named after the Northern Ireland politician, a winner of the Nobel Peace Prize and a graduate of the college.

'What's going on here?' he enquired.

The answer the inquisitive Ukrainian got was not what he had expected. 'Two of Ireland's leading sportsmen are receiving honorary doctorates,' he was told.

'Sportsmen?'

'Yes. Golfers.'

'Golfers? I don't understand. Why?'

'Because of the contribution they have made to Ireland, as sporting ambassadors, for their achievements, for their contributions to various charities.'

'I don't understand. They are golfers. Why should they get honorary doctorates?'

'I suppose,' he was told, 'it would be like Andriy Shevchenko being honoured in Ukraine.'

'We wouldn't.'

And, with that, he moved away, seemingly unimpressed and failing to understand what all the fuss was about, failing to understand the merits of Paul McGinley and Padraig Harrington being conferred with Degrees of Doctors of Arts, *honoris causa*, for, as Professor John G. Hughes, the President of NUI, Maynooth, put it, 'Their outstanding contributions to the sport of golf and for the distinction they have brought to Ireland by their achievements.'

At this time, there was no sign of McGinley or Harrington. It was only later, once the crowd had been ushered into the auditorium, that the two golfers, complete with red and white robes, entered behind a trail of academics that was led by Dr Attracta Halpin, the Registrar of the National University of Ireland. The two golfers seemed fazed, even bewildered. But they were smiling too, enjoying the pomp and ceremony of the occasion. As they looked up towards the lecture hall, they could pick out familiar faces, those of family and friends. It was the sort of assembly more likely to be found at a wedding.

Greg Allen, the golf commentator with RTÉ, Ireland's national broadcaster, provided the citation for the two men who grew up in Rathfarnham, a suburb of Dublin. He recalled how they attended the same school, Coláiste Éanna, and how, despite an age gap of five years, McGinley being the older, the two had bonded together through their feats on the golf course, of how they teamed-up to become winners of the World Cup at Kiawah Island in South Carolina in 1997, and of how the two were to play winning roles in the Ryder Cup matches of 2002 and 2004.

Unlike many modern day golfers, Allen was to point out to the assembly, that McGinley and Harrington were to obtain third level degrees before hitting the world's fairways. McGinley secured business and marketing qualifications in Dublin and San Diego and also worked at the European Union headquarters in Brussels for a year before embarking on a professional career. Harrington was to become a qualified accountant before he, too, became a professional golfer.

'As individuals, friends, team-mates and partners, they consistently represent their country with honour and distinction in both success and defeat. They are both articulate, intelligent ambassadors for Ireland in one of the world's most popular sports. Paul, in particular, living in England as he does, wears his Irishness in a manner which he himself acknowledges is the preserve of ex-pats, right down to marking his ball with the colours of the Irish flag, not to mention the green, white and orange wristbands and head covers,' Allen was to tell those gathered in the John Hume Building, moments before Dr Garret Fitzgerald, the Chancellor of NUI Maynooth and a former Taoiseach (Prime Minister) of Ireland, dramatically bowed to each golfer in turn and conferred on each an honorary doctorate, and requested that they sign the University Roll.

·   ·   ·   ·

TOM LEHMAN AND IAN WOOSNAM were among those playing in the Smurfit European Open. This time, the tournament, one of the flagship events on the PGA European Tour, was being played on the Smurfit Course, rather than the Palmer Course, on the north side of the River Liffey, that would play host to the Ryder Cup. Each was there to play in the tournament, but each captain had his mind on the Ryder Cup and how their respective teams were evolving.

Lehman, it seemed, was involved in some kind of psychological warfare that week. Or was he really serious in putting the underdogs tag on his own team?

'I'd say we're underdogs, without question,' he contended, even back then. 'I think we're underdogs in the fact that we've gotten thumped quite regularly over the last decade but, even looking at the world rankings today, I think there's more of the European players who are ranked in the top 25 than our American players.'

In actual fact, he was wrong. On that July day, there were more Americans (eight) in the world's top-25 than Europeans (seven). But it was a close-run thing, to be sure, and his point was taken. On this latest visit to The K Club, where he had taken to fishing for trout on the banks of the Liffey and to walking the course in the evening with his son, Sean, Lehman was on a public relations exercise and was heaping praise on to the Europeans.

'I see the European team as being very strong, and I see the American team as being in transition yet also very strong. There's a number of players who I have an incredible amount of faith in, a lot of confidence in … I'm not afraid of taking a bunch of inexperienced guys to play. I really am not. I have a great amount of confidence in their abilities and, more than anything else, these young guys are really hungry. They are really motivated to be part of this team and you can't replace the attitude of guys who have a bit of a competitive chip on their shoulders.

'It's a great way to play golf, with something to prove. So, being the underdog is no bad place for us to be. It's unusual, but I don't mind it. My own career has been that way. I've always been the kind of guy who's been overlooked and a bit of an underdog, so I don't mind playing from that direction at all,' said the US captain.

Lehman was referring to the positions occupied in his team by Brett Wetterich, Vaughn Taylor, Lucas Glover, JJ Henry and Zach Johnson. None of them had previously played in the most pressurised event in golf, although Lehman did point out that there were a number of big-money events, including the British Open and the US PGA, coming up which could yet alter his team standings. Was it wishful thinking?

Although Lehman had suggested to many of his potential team members that it might be a good idea to include the European Open on their itinerary, as he had done, none of them took up the proposal. 'I think because this tournament is not being held on the other course this year had a huge impact on the fact that nobody decided to come and play,' said Lehman.

In the days before the European Open got under way, his opposite number, Woosnam, could look at the field and know that most of those players likely to figure in his team for the match in September were present. He had decided, however, not to have any formal get-togethers, preferring instead to skip across to the Palmer Course to work out with the resort superintendent Gerry Byrne what condition the course would be in for the Ryder Cup. As home captain, it is his prerogative to suggest what speed the greens should be, or how deep the rough should be.

Back in May, when talking at the Irish Open, Woosnam had suggested that he would need a back door to slip out of Ireland should his team lose the match. Here, in July, he was very relaxed. His team was taking shape, and he liked it. On top of that, the American team as it stood had a plethora of novices, many of whom hadn't even played outside of the United States. Back in March at the Players Championship, Lehman issued a letter to prospective team members recommending that they add the European Open to their schedules and take the chance to pay a visit to the Ryder Cup venue. Not one of them took him up on the suggestion.

Woosnam was diplomatic when questioned on how the American team was shaping up. 'As things stand at the moment, I think we've got a big advantage. Yes. But, you know, these guys are great players and they can adapt to anything really, so we'll have to wait and see.'

With his own team evolving, Woosnam could consider bringing some of them together that week for a 'couple of beers and a chat.' There wasn't to be any organised dinner, though.

'Over the last four weeks, the team has really changed. We have some players I wanted in there, which is great ... [but] a couple of guys are struggling; García and McGinley, a little bit. I'd like to see them actually playing better. But I think our team is shaping up really well. There's going to be a lot of experience in there,' he explained.

At the BMW Championship at Wentworth in May, Woosnam had wondered out loud what on earth was happening when, as Europe's Ryder Cup captain, he could be paired with two Argentinian players for the first two rounds. Since then, the tour had orchestrated the draw so that he could play with and assess potential members of his team in the tournaments that Woosie played in. In the European Open, he was paired with McGinley for the first two rounds. The Irishman had been struggling with his form, but Woosnam was encouraging, and said:

'I think I'll put my arms around his shoulder and have a little talk to him, to just tell him to keep doing what he's doing. The game of golf can change in one week, so I'll just try to give him a bit of encouragement really. He just needs to hit a few good shots.'

· · · ·

THE SMILES ON THE FACES of Harrington and McGinley as they enjoyed a day away from the golf course and the practice range on 10 July was not just because they were being honoured that day—it also had to do with the fact that each player, through their on-course deeds of the previous days and weeks, had strengthened their claims for automatic places on the European team for the Ryder Cup at The K Club, just about six miles away from the university as the crow flies.

Harrington had all but sealed his automatic place by finishing second in the previous week's French Open at the National Club in Paris, a tournament he had only added on to his schedule after a request from European team captain Woosnam, worried that so many of his so-called 'big hitters' had not yet played their way into an automatic place on the team. It was to prove to be a wise move, and was the end part of a midsummer's run of form that also saw Harrington finish fifth in the US Open at Winged Foot and second in the following week's tournament on the PGA Tour, the Booz Allen Classic in Washington, before his performance in France.

On conferring day, McGinley's mood was a stark contrast to that of the previous Friday when he finished the second round of the Smurfit European Open at The K Club's Smurfit Course. The Palmer Course was already being groomed in preparation for the big one, some two and a half months later.

After removing his spikes and emerging from the player's locker-room in the Smurfit Clubhouse on the Friday, McGinley had the look of a man consigned to his fate. Earlier in the season, during the Nissan Irish Open at Carton House, he had withdrawn from the tournament to undergo knee surgery that was carried out by Dr Ray Moran, one of Ireland's leading surgeons and a brother of former Ireland and Manchester United soccer international, Kevin.

The injury, which first occurred 20 years before when McGinley broke a kneecap playing Gaelic football, and which necessitated surgery in November 2004, had led to so much discomfort that it was affecting his ability to play shots. So it was that he took the bigger picture decision to withdraw from the Irish Open, his home tournament, and book into the Cappagh Hospital in Finglas for immediate surgery.

However, although the knee surgery was considered a success, it took a number of weeks out of McGinley's schedule and he had come into the Smurfit European Open struggling with his game. After signing for a second round score of 71 for 146, two-over, he was positioned in tied-88th and well outside the cut line which each week on tour falls at 65th position-plus ties.

His mood was one of despondency, resigned to missing another cut in a thus-far wretched season.

'What can I say? Nothing's going right. The problem is I am off form. I made the Ryder Cup team the very hard way the last time [in 2004]. The pressure of making the team is something that I have dealt with twice before. I have just got to keep going. Mentally I'm tired. I'm running out of confidence and ideas in myself,' said McGinley.

As it happened, Woosnam was also standing in the hallway of the clubhouse and overheard McGinley bearing his soul. The Dubliner's lack of form was reflected in the statistic that he was fourth in the world points list and second in the European points list on January 3rd in Europe's qualifying tables and now, in early July, had dropped to 13th in the world list and to eighth in the European list.

'Every week it goes on, it gets more difficult for Paul,' said Woosnam. 'You've got to remember that he is still in the team at the moment. He's just got to have patience. He's also experienced enough to put too much pressure on himself. It is just one of those things, you can try too hard. You've just got to stay focused.'

There was to be a touch of prophecy about Woosnam's words, but even he could hardly have known how soon he was to be proven right. McGinley headed off to Dublin Airport convinced that he would miss the cut at the European Open and, as he drove down the M50 motorway, he would not have noticed that the winds were picking up considerably.

McGinley went through the routine of preparing to travel home to his home in Sunningdale, booking on to his Aer Lingus flight to London Heathrow. It was only when he was in the lounge, waiting to board the plane, that he got a call from his wife, Alison, who advised him that the cut mark had risen since he had finished his round and that he should seriously consider not embarking the plane. At this stage, McGinley's luggage and golf clubs had already been loaded onto the aircraft but, on explaining his position, the Aer Lingus staff delayed the plane so that his gear could be retrieved. McGinley, himself, was to play golf over the weekend at The K Club like a man reprieved.

· · · ·

When McGinley's golf clubs were removed from Aer Lingus Flight EI169 on the Friday evening at Dublin Airport and returned with him to The K Club for the third round on the Saturday morning, the player still had much work to do if he was to earn a decent pay cheque and, with it, the euros that constitute a point for each unit of the currency claimed in the European points list.

After all, McGinley's form left a lot to be desired and there had been no recent evidence that he could turn it around. His win in the Volvo Masters, the season-ending championship at the end of the 2005 European Tour, had provided McGinley with his biggest single input to the qualifying campaign but he had failed to muster even one top-10 finish on tour since he had undergone knee surgery in May.

Stephen Dodd, of Wales, was to win the Smurfit European Open; but, to those gathered in the giant grandstand and standing on grassy banks all around the Smurfit Course, the big winner was McGinley. To the Irish spectators who flocked to the course over the weekend, McGinley's revival wasn't akin to Lazarus rising from the dead; but it was close. His transformation from the brink of despair on Friday evening when he travelled to Dublin airport believing he had missed the cut, to weekend rounds of 67 and 69 that catapulted him through the field to eventually finish in tied-fourth and brought that wide grin of his back to his face, constituted a modern day epiphany to indicate some form of divine inspiration.

On the Sunday, a stiff crosswind blew across the hillocks on the southern side of the Liffey, causing many players to struggle with club selection and ball control and expanding the stroke average in the final round to 75.46, Dodd, of those who started the day in contention, was the only one to remain immune from trouble. His response to two early round blips, back-to-back bogeys at the sixth and seventh, was to cover the remaining 11 holes in four-under, eventually finishing with a 70 for 279, nine-under, two shots clear of runners-up Anthony Wall, who sank a 35-footer for birdie on the last, and José Manuel Lara.

Dodd covered the back nine in 33 strokes, and McGinley, four groups ahead of the Welshman, was the only one to match that homeward run. When the Irishman rolled in a seven-footer for birdie on the 18th, a putt he reckoned was more difficult that the one that made him a Ryder Cup hero at the Belfry in 2002 as it had a double break—right-to-left and left-to-right—he assumed the clubhouse lead and was in a share of second place, just one shot off the then leader.

The logjam was such that a play-off was conceivable, and McGinley headed to the practice range just in case. But Dodd's finish, a bogey-free back nine that included birdies at the 11th, 16th and 17th, enabled him to escape clear of Wall, who birdied the last, and Lara, who had birdied the 16th and 17th to recover from three dropped shots in successive holes from the 12th.

Quite rightly, though, McGinley was proud of his weekend's work, where he finished in tied-fourth on 282 alongside Lee Westwood, Graeme Storm, Simon Khan and Jeev Mikha Singh.

'If flight EI169 hadn't been delayed on Friday night, I'd have been flying over The K Club, not playing on it,' he quipped of an evening spent waiting in an airport lounge with too much time to think of the fates that had befallen him.

On Saturday, in the third round, McGinley hit 17 greens in regulation and was just on the fringe of the one he missed, the fourth. Afterwards, he was to reflect: 'That's normally my game. I wear the golf course down, by hitting fairways and hitting greens. It is nice to see my game back. It is a while since I played with confidence.'

As the crowds finally dispersed from the southern side of the Liffey at The K Club, they were basking in the glow of McGinley's apparent return to form, even if it was a Welshman who had won the actual title. It was another Welshman, Woosnam not Dodd, that McGinley threw accolades to.

'Woosie's been great. He had a word in my ear. He was supportive and wasn't on my case. He did everything a captain should do and his role as Ryder Cup captain has really started in earnest with a lot of players jostling for position.

'This is going to be the strongest European team ever because the standard on tour now is so incredibly high and there is so many players capable of making the team. Plus the guys who made the team the last time with a record victory in Oakland Hills, we all want to be on it as well, allied to the guys coming up from behind. I think it is going to be a hell of a strong team.'

· · · ·

THE DAY AFTER THE NIGHT before, McGinley's smile was still on his face. He was standing in the corridors of St Patrick's College in NUI Maynooth. On either wall in this grand, old hallway are photographs of a bygone age, of priests who graduated from this august college, many of them who went on to become bishops and cardinals. The recently conferred Dr Paul McGinley was anxious to dispel the impression that he had booked his place on Woosnam's Ryder Cup team. He was throwing out words of caution, warning that there was still much work to be done.

'No, the job's not done. I am going to put out the signal very strongly that I've got to keep going forward and that I want to make the team. I don't want to stumble over the line, I want to make the team running. I want to sprint over the line,' said McGinley, glass of wine in one hand. The other hand was required to keep up the endless number of handshakes that were coming his way, from well-wishers thrilled not only that he has been afforded the honorary doctorate an hour or so beforehand, but that his deeds in the Smurfit European Open over the weekend that had gone a long ways towards securing his place on the team for the Ryder Cup.

The Dubliner had strengthened his claims for an automatic place on Europe's team by moving up to seventh in the composite table, taken from the world points and European points lists. He didn't intend to slacken off, reminding those around him that he intended to play in the Barclay's Scottish Open, the British Open and the Deutsche Bank over the following three weeks.

'I don't want to give the guys behind any impression that I am slacking off,' he said.

His relentless pursuit of points was part of the grand plan to make a third successive Ryder Cup team, and came after a weekend's performance at The K Club that ignited his season. Standing in the hallway, replete in robes, McGinley attributed his turnaround in fortunes to a swing tip given to him on the range prior to the tournament by his coach, Bob Torrance.

'I was thinking about it this morning as I was brushing my teeth. If there was one key, it was working with Bob on something very different, just changing my ball flight to give more penetration; particularly in the wind.'

The key had come in the gathering dusk of the Tuesday evening before the tournament on the range at Straffan. Those late-night vigils on the range had been familiar to McGinley in recent weeks as he sought something to transform his season. At Gleneagles a few weeks previously, having arrived there after missing the cut in the US Open, he could be seen on the range until the sun had gone down.

The same was true at the French Open, the week before his metamorphosis at The K Club. A sports fanatic, and a season ticket holder at both Celtic and West Ham, McGinley is not one to miss out on watching a good football match. But on the night of the France-Brazil match in the World Cup, McGinley preferred working on the putting green at Paris National rather than watching the game on television.

'I was on the putting green in the darkness looking for that little spark, and I could hear the roars going up all around Paris.'

On the eve of the final round at The K Club, McGinley attended a barbecue. If he'd missed the cut and caught his flight home the previous night, he wouldn't have had the chance to talk with DJ Carey, a legendary hurler who had guided Kilkenny to countless All-Ireland hurling titles and who was also enjoying some Irish steak and grilled vegetables. The two talked of sports' peaks and troughs, of the ebb and flow of form. Earlier that day, McGinley had played his best round of golf of the season. To the golfer, it was like prising open a door that had been shut in his face.

'There is a large weight off my mind that I've produced quality golf again. From here on in it is about reproducing it. The point is,' he said, 'I haven't lost it. The point is, that I can play quality golf and that I can compete.'

McGinley's goal from early in the year had been to make the European Ryder Cup team, to be a part of the biggest international sporting event ever to be staged in his home country. Probably the biggest that ever would be staged, as people were viewing it then.

'I don't want to be in the team playing poorly. I don't want to be in the team and the captain having to worry about me and me having to worry about myself. I want to be in the team like I was at Oakland Hills, where I earned my spot and was able to stand toe-to-toe with anyone in the team knowing that I had earned my spot.

'There's a lot more pressure on picks than people give credit for. Picks haven't earned it as much as the first 10 guys and there is always pressure on the picks, and I want to be able to stand toe-to-toe knowing I have earned my spot. If I don't make it from here, I don't deserve to be in the team ... my goals haven't moved but at least I feel like I can achieve them now. I felt like I was swimming against the tide the last six months. I felt I was doing all the right things, playing a lot of reasonable golf, but not scoring.'

The events of the previous few days had strengthened McGinley's quest for an automatic place on Woosnam's team. Little did he know that his place wouldn't be confirmed until the very last qualifying tournament, the BMW International in Munich. On this day though, it was about celebrating his honorary doctorate.

'It's a very, very nice thing,' said McGinley. 'To share it with Padraig is especially nice. We have done so many things together throughout our lives. We're joined at the hip to a large extent.'

Dr Harrington, too, felt that way. 'It's definitely made the day that bit more special, that it has been done with Paul. It brings home how much we've been linked over the years. Paul was a big role model when I was at school because, as I like to point out, he is five years older than me. When I got to school, he was just leaving. But his was the big name in terms of golf.'

But that day in July was not just about the two golfers, it was also about remembering Harrington's father. Paddy Harrington, who died almost twelve months to the day previously, was his son's guiding force. He introduced the young Padraig to golf when he was five years of age, and taught him many of life's lessons. On this day, the Paddy Harrington Golf Scholarships had been launched and Padraig Harrington exuded pride in this.

'Junior golf was very close to my dad's heart. He would love to have been a coach, not in golf, a life coach. He was always into the coaching end of things, the mental side of things, he'd have been very pleased about any scholarship and a scholarship to carry his name is a very proud moment for me and my family. He would have loved anything to encourage young kids, for them to get an education with their golf game so that they are not one dimensional.'

SIX

In Memory of Earl

Liverpool, England. July 2006.

IN DETERMINING THE TEAMS FOR the Ryder Cup, no tournament has as much influence as a major championship. The qualifying system used by the United States gives added weight, and more points, to top-ten finishes in majors. Under the dual qualifying system used by Europe, one offering world ranking points accumulated over a twelve month period and the other based on one point for each euro won, performing well at a major championship can be worth its weight in gold.

So it was that anyone with aspirations of playing at The K Club in September turned up at Royal Liverpool Golf Club in July for the third major of the season, the 135th Open Championship. The links at Hoylake, being used for the first time since 1967 as a host course for the British Open, offered quite a contrast to either Augusta National or Winged Foot, the previous major venues in 2006. There was no lush grass to be found here. In fact, the fescue grasses had been burned to a wisp and the ground underfoot was like concrete.

The Open is unique amongst all the majors, in that spectators can pay their entrance money at the gates. On this occasion, they were greeted with requests from marshals not to light up cigarettes or discard bottles on the sand dunes for fear of causing fires, so parched were the links. It all seemed a far cry from the famed old links that originally doubled as a horse racing track and which was once described by the legendary golf writer Bernard Darwin as, 'Hoylake, blown by mighty winds, breeder of mighty champions.' This week, there was barely a breath of wind.

In more recent times, the golf course designer Donald Steel had been asked to toughen up the course so that the Royal and Ancient Golf Club of St Andrews, who annually run the Open, would once again include it on the championship rota. Steel added an extra 263 yards to the course that was played in 1967, refurnished the course's 94 bunkers, built three new tees and reshaped several greens.

'Hoylake will always be Hoylake, I'm simply rearranging the furniture,' he was to remark ahead of the championship.

And it was here that Tiger Woods came, playing in his first major since missing the cut at the US Open in June. During the Smurfit Kappa European Open the previous month, Tom Lehman, the US captain, had been asked of his concerns about Woods, whose father, Earl, had died in May.

'I wish I knew the answer to that. I think Tiger's father was always the guy that you could go to, no matter what the situation or no matter what the circumstance to give him the straight truth and that perfect advice he needed. I don't know how you replace someone like that. You can have all kinds of great friends around you and a great wife and everything, but there's no way to replace what you lost.'

Lehman's concerns about Woods, already guaranteed a place on the US team for the Ryder Cup match at The K Club, were similar to those he harboured about Chris DiMarco. In the 2005 President's Cup, DiMarco, a passionate and exuberant player, had been the on-course inspiration for the United States' win over the Rest of the World team, a side that nonetheless excluded Europeans. DiMarco had forged an impressive partnership with Phil Mickelson but, at this point in time in July, he was not in an automatic qualifying position for the Ryder Cup. Furthermore, he was playing in Hoylake just three weeks after the sudden death of his mother, Norma.

DiMarco was one player that Lehman did not want to use as a captain's 'wild card' pick. He wanted him to qualify by right. 'Chris has always brought to the team a huge amount of enthusiasm, a lot of emotion. He's a fun guy to be around and he's very passionate about the things that he loves.'

One of the pursuits other than golf that DiMarco engages in is skiing. Back in February, he had told Lehman he was going on a skiing vacation. 'Don't go skiing, just don't going skiing,' was Lehman's reaction. The captain went so far as to call DiMarco's friend who was to accompany the player. 'Tell DiMarco if he blows out his knee, I'm going to break his neck.'

DiMarco didn't break his knee. He broke his rib, and was struggling to regain form that had him, as Lehman succinctly put it, 'behind the eight-ball' in terms of qualifying for the team by the time he got to Hoylake.

The bond that exists between golfers is a common one, and strong. While Woods and DiMarco had shared family bereavements, their thoughts were also very much with Darren Clarke. The Northern Irishman's wife, Heather, had been battling cancer for a number of years but she had urged Clarke to continue playing. His schedule was a stop-start one for much of the season but he, too, made his way to Hoylake in the quest for a major that had frustratingly eluded him on a number of occasions in recent years.

On the eve of the championship, Woods, who ironically had formed a close friendship with Clarke when losing to the cigar-smoking Ulsterman in the final of the Accenture Match Play in 2000, a friendship that grew closer with each year, took time out to comment on Clarke's ability to contend in the tournaments that he had played in throughout 2006 and all the while worrying about his wife's ailing health.

'You know, the fact that Darren's been in contention the last couple of weeks has been absolutely remarkable. God, the things he is going through … I truly feel for him because it's not fun for anyone to watch someone you love deteriorate right in front of you, and they're not the person they used to be, and they can't do the things that they normally are accustomed to doing.

'You watch that each and every day, it's very, very difficult to handle … the way he's dealt with it, with playing and competing, has been remarkable. It shows the character and type of person that he is. And, as a friend, to watch him go through it, my heart goes out to him and his entire family. He's a remarkable man, and so is Heather, a remarkable person,' Woods empathised with the Clarkes.

Clarke delayed his arrival on The Wirral until only shortly before the championship to give him time to return to his London home from Scotland where he had competed the previous week. He wanted to spend as much time as he could with his wife. He still contended more often than not (especially in the Irish Open and the Scottish Open) only to fail to finish the job at the business end of proceedings.

Of Clarke's inability to close out, Woods was to remark, 'It's draining, it's very draining. I don't know if it's a mechanical problem in his game, or is it just his mental edge, or just not getting the right breaks at the right time … but, in any case, just for him to be out here playing and in contention, hats off to him.'

In the early part of the season, Clarke had taken to working with Ewen Murray, the Sky Sports golf commentator, who had given him some advice that enabled the player to consistently get into contention in tournaments. However, a title win was proving elusive, as epitomised by his fall-off in the final round of the Barclays Scottish Open at Loch Lomond on the Sunday before Hoylake when Clarke had finished fifth.

Not unlike Clarke, Woods' season had been a disrupted one, with only nine appearances on tour up to his arrival in Hoylake. But he had won on two occasions, in the Buick Invitational and the Doral Championship, while finishing second in the Western Open in Chicago in his warm-up tournament before heading to England for the British Open.

Woods' outings since the US Masters in April had been rare. After Winged Foot, he didn't reappear until the Western Open as he sought to come to terms, firstly, with his father's illness and, then, his death. Rather than undertake his traditional visit to Ireland in the week before the British Open, Woods decided to remain home in Orlando, Florida, to work on some aspects of his game.

It is traditional for Woods to prepare for British Opens by not only playing links golf, but also assiduously watching videos of old championships. In the case of Hoylake, however, there were no old videos to watch. So, Woods arrived a couple of days earlier than is his custom, touching down in his private jet in Liverpool on Saturday and immediately making his way to the course. He was keenly aware that his nemesis, Phil Mickelson, had already spent a considerable amount of time visiting Hoylake and learning the nuances of the links.

Woods probably wasn't too impressed with the draw for the first two rounds, which had put him in the same group as Nick Faldo who, in his role as a television analyst on US television, was once highly critical of Woods' swing.

'Will you be talking [with Nick] on Thursday and Friday?' Woods was asked beforehand.

'I've only played with him two times since I've been a pro and there wasn't a lot of talking there, either,' was Woods' response, adding: 'I'll be in my world trying to compete and trying to win the championship, and I'm sure he'll probably do the same thing.'

• • • •

ON FRIDAY AFTERNOON, 21 JULY, Darren Clarke took 82 strokes to get around the links at Hoylake. He missed the cut. Not long after his last, horrid shot of a day when he must have wondered what on earth he was doing playing golf, Clarke announced that he would not be competing again for the foreseeable future as he would be spending time with his wife, and two children, Tyrone and Conor.

Clarke was not alone to suffer the wrath of Hoylake. Paul McGinley, who had been hovering on the mark for much of the afternoon and into the late evening, failed to make the cut by one shot after US Ryder Cup prospect Vaughn Taylor, in the fourth from last group, birdied the 18th to bring the cut from level to one-under. Other heavyweight casualties included Padraig Harrington, Colin Montgomerie, David Howell and the Americans Fred Couples and Davis Love. John Daly, too, spectacularly missed the cut when, two-under playing the last, he put two balls out-of-bounds at a time when caution would have been far more prudent a course of action.

Taylor was one of those players who had played his way into contention for a place on Lehman's Ryder Cup team. He was also one of a number of American players who hadn't even owned a passport until his form on the PGA Tour indicated that maybe it might be a good idea to go and get one.

'The Ryder is a big goal. I'm just trying to take it week by week and not to get ahead of myself. I just feel like if I go through my routine and just take it week by week then everything will kind of take care of itself,' he said at the time.

Although hailing from Augusta, Taylor had not grown up crafting his game on the manicured fairways of Augusta National.

'I just came from a middle class family and just basically worked pretty hard to get where I am. I wasn't a world beater at the start.

I've felt like I've gotten better each year, just worked my way up. Tom [Lehman] said it kind of reminded him of his own career and himself ... I've never really received a lot of attention, I always tend to kind of fly in under the radar.'

Graeme McDowell had carried the first round lead into the second day's play, believing perhaps that there is such a thing as fate. The only Irishman ever to win an Open Championship was Fred Daly in 1947 and he had achieved the feat on this same Hoylake links. But, for much of the day, the roars that resonated around the dunes on this piece of golfing terrain on Merseyside were those indicating a different fate as Tiger Woods, just like old times, was strutting his stuff. Each deed, including audaciously holing out with his second shot for an eagle two on the 14th hole, was greeted with royal and ancient acclaim.

To all and sundry, it seemed that Woods was on an unstoppable and predestined route to further major glory. It looked to be all over, bar the shouting. But golf is rarely such a walk in the park and, late-on in the second round, there was sufficient evidence from familiar adversaries, among them Ernie Els, to indicate that this 135th Open Championship would be no one-man-show.

When the dust had settled on an absorbing day's golf, Woods was indeed positioned as the leader after a second round 65 left him on 12-under-par 132, just two strokes adrift of the record low 36-holes total achieved by Nick Faldo at Muirfield in 1992. But the world's number one had only to cast a glance over his shoulder to find the resurgent figure of Els, emerging from the competitive doldrums to lie one shot behind heading into the weekend's play.

Woods was not the only American to shine. DiMarco, finding inspiration from somewhere so shortly after the death of his mother, also recorded a new course record of 65. The player with the distinctive claw-putting grip claimed that the only reason he was even playing was because that is what his mother would have wanted.

'Walking between the ropes is absolutely therapeutic for me,' he was to say.

For Woods, it was one of those days when more things go right than wrong. On the 14th, with 194 yards to the front of the green, he hit a four-iron approach that found the bottom of the hole for an eagle two. It was the highlight of a round that featured an eagle, six birdies and a single bogey.

There may not have been much conversation taking place between them on the course, but Faldo, who played alongside Woods, foresaw only one winner.

'His touch is so good, his competitive ability the best, I would predict he could get to 20-under. How are they going to beat him with that score? He's got a great game plan, playing so many irons.'

Faldo's sentiment was shared by McGinley, who repeated his pre-championship assertion that, 'The guy with the most skill is going to play the best around here, and Tiger has the most skill of anybody in the world. You've got to work the ball, you've got to manipulate it. You've got to shape it off those tight lies, and you've got to work it into the wind and have a good short game. He's the best player in the world.'

So, it was a case of back to normal for Woods. He was still, unquestionably the best front runner in golf, refusing to let his thoughts get ahead of him as he entered the weekend seeking to retain the trophy he had won at St Andrews in 2005.

'I'm not here with the jug,' he said to the gathering in the media centre. 'We've got 36 holes to go. Unless there's some kind of rain storm coming in and it is cancelled after two days, we have a long way to go yet.'

•   •   •   •

THE RAINS NEVER DID COME to Hoylake in July, neither did the storms, and nobody did manage to catch Woods. As he went about reclaiming the old claret jug with an imperious performance on the links, the only possible disruption to his reign came when a disaffected spectator, claiming to represent a group calling for fathers' rights, threw some flour bombs onto the 18th green that left purple hues on the final green. They were to be the only stain on a final day's romp to glory.

All day, until his last putt, the 270th stroke of the championship, fell into the tin cup on the 18th green, Woods had played with a steely determination. It was flawless golf, without a hint of any frailty. Then, as the Nike ball plonked into the hole for a final time, it all came home to him. The well of emotion erupted, and tears streamed down Woods' face. When he'd won his previous ten majors, his father, his mentor and guiding light, had been on hand to share the joy. This time, as his caddie Steve Williams indicated by pointing to the heavens above this parched terrain on Merseyside, Woods Senior had a different view of his son's superiority over the golfing world.

The tears wouldn't stop, and Woods threw his arms around his friend and bagman Williams and used the giant New Zealander as a comforter.

'I've never done that [before]. With all the things we've gone through of late … I guess I'm the kind of one who bottles things up a little bit and moves on, tries to deal with things in my own way. But, at that moment, it just came pouring out; of all the things my father has meant to me and the game of golf,' Woods explained. In truth, his words didn't need to be spoken. His actions had done all the talking.

This 11th major win of his career had moved him up to second, alongside Walter Hagen, in the all-time list of major winners and moved him closer to the record 18 held by Jack Nicklaus. It was a performance of clinical precision, his final round 67 giving him a

72-holes total of 270, 18-under, and a two strokes winning margin over his fellow-American DiMarco.

Others with aspirations to claim the title flattered only to deceive. Els finished alone in third after a 71 (for 275), and Jim Furyk, the player ear-marked to be Woods' right-hand-man for the Ryder Cup, took fourth place with a 71 (for 276). But Sergio García, paired together with Woods in the final twosome, and tasked with attempting to end the European drought in the majors which dated back to 1999, failed to make any worthwhile challenge and eventually required a birdie at the 15th and eagle at the 16th simply to claim a share of fifth place, finishing with a 73 (for 277).

It was an emotional day too for DiMarco, who said: 'I know how my mom would be very proud of me right now. One, for playing well. But, two, because that's just how she was. I miss her and I love her and I have great memories of her. That's the hardest part, to know I'll never see her again. But I know if I close my eyes, I see here. She is and was a wonderful woman. There is a lot of family support. It just helps knowing that she was a big part out there today, and I know I'll have her here with me for the rest of my life.'

DiMarco may not have won, but he had the consolation of a runner-up finish that enabled him to move from 21st to sixth in the United States Ryder Cup standings. He had benefited enormously from the increased weighting given to majors and this spectacular return to form confirmed his place in the team for the Ryder Cup match. Lehman, more than anyone, was happy with that fact. He wouldn't have to use one of his 'wild card' picks on DiMarco after all.

Of all the current crop of American players, DiMarco is the one most obviously buoyed by the prospect of team golf. His fist-pumps with Mickelson in the President's Cup became a trademark.

But his only previous experience in the Ryder Cup, like so many of his peers, had been of losing.

'Obviously, winning a major would always solidify your career, there's no doubt about that ... [but] playing for your country is probably the greatest thing I've ever done in golf. So I'd have to say playing for the country [would mean more than winning a major]. It would mean that much for me to come back here and go to The K Club and be part of that team. Once you've been on a team, you don't want to miss any. It's nice that my form is back with some weeks to go,' DiMarco was to claim.

On a final day when the wind accentuated the challenge of a parched links, DiMarco was the only player to make life difficult for Woods. But even he failed to chase down golf's most dominant player, as he reflected:

'If you can't get up to playing the best player in the world in a major, I don't know what else there is. It pumps me up. I know Tiger once said being in contention in a major is like a drug. And it is. It is our drug. It is so awesome to be playing well and performing well when everything is on the line. As a player it is the best thing in the world.'

In the end, Woods could afford the luxury of a par on the last hole to win a title he claimed meant more to him that his previous British Open successes, both of which came at St Andrews (in 2000 and 2005).

The explanation for Woods' display of emotion on the 18th green, a genuine and heart-felt outpouring of his emotions, had all to do with his father's absence.

'Basically, to win your first tournament after your father has passed away, and for it to be a major championship, makes it that bit more special,' he was to remark.

The manner of his win, the way he hit one perfect shot after another, was an example to everyone in sport, not just golf. Woods stuck with a strategy that saw him use the driver just once in 72 holes, and was subsequently to comment that his father would have been 'very, very proud' of the way that he stuck to his game plan which had been conceived early in the week when he arrived to find a parched links that required strategic placement off the tee rather than brute force.

'He was always on my case about thinking my way around the golf course and not letting emotions get the better of you, because it is very easy to do in this sport … and just to use your mind to plot your way around the golf course and, if you had to deviate from the game plan, to make sure it is the right decision to do that. He was very adamant I play like that my entire playing career. With the golf course being this fast, it lent itself to just being amazing creatively … these were the most difficult pins I've ever seen at an Open championship. The only defence they had was pin locations and hard, dry conditions.'

Of those seeking to usurp Woods' reign, DiMarco had made the best fist of it. Although he bogeyed the first, it was to be the only dropped shot he suffered as he gamely battled for that elusive maiden major. DiMarco secured birdies at the sixth, 10th, 13th, 16th and 18th holes and also showed tenacity by saving par whenever he got into trouble, demonstrated by his up-and-down from heavy rough on the 14th where he holed a 40-footer to keep the pressure on Woods.

Woods, who had sank a 15-footer for eagle on the fifth, moved three ahead of his nearest pursuer DiMarco by birdying the 10th. His only error of the round came when he dropped a shot on the 12th, with DiMarco, in the match ahead, almost simultaneously getting a birdie on the 13th when he holed from 20 feet. The margin between the two at that stage was reduced to just one shot, but Woods' reaction was masterly. He grabbed a hat-trick of birdies from the 14th, and drove home the message that nobody was tugging the claret jug from his grasp.

Unlike other players who claim not to look at scoreboards, Woods looked at each and every one.

'I was aware of what Chris and Ernie were doing up ahead of me. Chris made a little bit of a run on that back nine. He kept pushing me. Luckily, I was able to make three in a row to give myself a chance to get some breathing space,' admitted Woods.

DiMarco has gone head-to-head in majors before with Woods, in the 2005 US Masters when he lost in a play-off and had also witnessed his conqueror hole an unbelievable chip at the 16th hole of the final round, and stepped up to the plate again here. It was not to be, however.

'Tiger's got an uncanny ability to just turn it up to another level, when somebody gets close to him … it's just hard to catch him,' was DiMarco's post-championship assessment.

Yet again, Woods had demonstrated his mastery. He arrived at Hoylake unsure of how to play the course but, after hitting some drivers in practice, felt it would be best to leave the club in the bag. In fact, he used it just once in four days, on the 16th hole of Thursday's first round. 'I developed a strategy to play this golf course that I thought suited me and I felt comfortable with. I went out there and executed my game plan. I adjusted clubs off the tees, just because the wind conditions kept changing, but as far as the overall game plan, I never deviated.'

Throughout the four rounds, Woods' superiority over the rest of the field was demonstrated with a sense of clinical strategy that emphasised finesse rather than force. He was first in fairways hit (85%) and second in greens-in-regulation (80%). Most importantly, he took fewer strokes than anyone to get the ball into the hole. In becoming the first player since Tom Watson in 1983 to successfully defend the Open championship, Woods just one shot shy of equalling his own low total of 19-under-par set at St Andrews in 2000. It was, truly, a masterful performance. It was the kind of performance that the United States would require, if he was to inspire his country to a first Ryder Cup win since the so-called 'Battle of Brookline' in 1999.

SEVEN

Tragedy

Chicago, United States. August 2006.

WHEN PAUL MCGINLEY'S MOBILE PHONE sounded in the early hours of Sunday morning, 13 August, he knew it was not good news. Moments later, his worst fears were confirmed. Heather Clarke had passed away. She was 39.

In that instant, he knew too there was only one possible decision for him to make. He would withdraw from that week's US PGA Championship at Medinah Golf Club, outside Chicago, so that he could attend the funeral in Northern Ireland, along with his wife, Alison, one of Heather's closest friends. Although his place on Europe's team was far from safe, this was a time to be with friends and family, not to be chasing Ryder Cup points.

Padraig Harrington was in the process of boarding a flight from Dublin to Chicago when he got the news that Heather Clarke had lost her long fight with breast cancer. Unsure of whether to stay in Dublin, getting the airline staff to retrieve his clubs and bags from the hold, or to travel with the option of returning home, Harrington decided to continue on with his journey. As it transpired, that is what Darren Clarke wanted him to do.

Other European players were going through similar emotions; Thomas Bjørn, Lee Westwood, Graeme McDowell. McDowell, who had spent the previous week at his new home in Florida but who had grown up playing and crafting his swing on the same windswept links courses on the Causeway Coast as his elder role model, was especially unsure of what to do. Ultimately, their decisions to play in the US PGA, the fourth and final major of the season, and a championship that could impact greatly on who would or wouldn't make the European team for the Ryder Cup match at The K Club the following month, were made for them by Clarke who insisted that, 'Heather would have wanted them to play.'

Harrington too had seriously considered returning home, but he was to be strongly influenced by Clarke's words. In the week of a major, Harrington would normally play a number of practice rounds with McGinley. This time, it would be different. But Harrington, who announced that he would donate any prize money he won in the PGA to a charity for breast cancer research, also understood the special relationship that existed between the Clarkes and the McGinleys. Their homes had backed onto each other in Sunningdale for many years, before the Clarkes moved house, but they had remained the closest of friends and their children attended the same schools.

While some, including Europe's captain Ian Woosnam, wondered if McGinley had over-reacted in the decision he had taken, Harrington had no such thoughts.

'There was no decision [for Paul to make]. For a decision, you have to sit down and think about it. It wasn't even close to a decision … Paul's in a different boat to us. With Ali, their lives are intertwined [with the Clarkes]. Things like this make you realise it really is only a game of golf and there's a lot more outside of it.'

Heather Clarke's death transcended team boundaries as Europeans and Americans alike grieved for her passing. On the morning of Thursday, 17 August, just over half an hour before the first tee shot would be played in the 88th US PGA Championship, a crowd of more than 100 people gathered on the putting green close to the huge, Byzantine clubhouse of Medinah Country

Club. It was 6.30am and precisely an hour before the scheduled funeral service of Heather Clarke six time zones away in Northern Ireland.

Tom Lehman looked out at the array of faces assembled on the putting green; Players, caddies, tour officials, media. All had come to pay their respects.

'There's competition and there's life and we should never, ever confuse the two. Never. Ever. There are way more important things, like the well-being of Darren Clarke and his family than any golf tournament … why at age 39 is she gone? Just like I wonder why Payne Stewart was taken from us?' Lehman told those gathered in front of him.

Lehman's words were gently spoken, just as they had been when he spoke at the memorial service in 1999 for his friend, Payne Stewart, who had died in a plane crash. This time, seven years on, speaking again about death, Lehman informed those listening to his words that there would be a time to finally get answers to those questions, and added: 'Know that God is still there, and he will comfort the broken-hearted.'

The first few groups, with players wearing black ribbons as a mark of respect, had started their rounds in the US PGA Championship when, on the other side of the Atlantic, Heather Clarke was laid to rest. In addressing the funeral service at Ballywillan Presbyterian Church, Rev. Jim Frazer, who had married Darren and Heather, told the golfer— sitting in the front pew of the church with his two sons, Tyrone and Conor—that on, 'That day in March 1996 when you married her here in this church, Darren, you really won the greatest trophy of your life. She was a lovely girl and a lovely person, unpretentious and without any guile at all. She was full of character.'

Rev. Frazer had continued: 'Growing up with two brothers, she quickly learnt how to handle men. She found it slightly more difficult handling Darren, however, but she quickly realised that if he was going to travel the world's golf courses with his friends, she would travel the world's shops with hers! The result was, when registering her death, in typical Clarke fashion, I gather he put: "Housewife/Serial Shopper!"… so for Darren, those words ring true today: Do not be sad for what you've lost. Be glad for what you had! Over the years, Heather faced the roller-coaster of her illness with a quiet determination and a grace that was characteristic of all she did. At the end, she was at peace, and early last Sunday morning, death came as a friend, and took her, and she was at rest.'

· · · ·

PROVIDING A FEW WORDS AT the prayer service on the first morning of the US PGA Championship was just one of Lehman's duties at Medinah. As US Ryder Cup captain, Lehman would, on the following Monday, be required to name his two 'wild card' picks for the match at The K Club. By then, depending on whatever happened in the season's final major, or 'Glory's Last Shot' as the PGA of America called it, the ten automatic places could have altered.

In a way, these were strange times for Lehman. On the previous Sunday, but for a little luck here and there, he could have won the International tournament in Colorado. If he'd won, Lehman would have moved up to seventh in the US team's qualifying. Instead, his runner-up finish to Dean Wilson after a play-off left him in 19th position going into the US PGA.

Ironically, Lehman's close call in the International also demonstrated the inherent weakness in the US qualifying system. After all, here was a player who had not won a tournament since the Phoenix Open in 2000, and who hadn't earned a single Ryder Cup point since the Accenture Matchplay the previous February, but who could still have secured an automatic place on the team by winning the International—basically one good performance all summer.

He didn't win, of course. Wilson, a six-time winner in Japan, claimed his maiden PGA Tour success. But it really was a case of 'what if?' for Lehman. What if the tournament had been played in the traditional strokeplay format rather than in the modified stableford system applied by organisers of the International? Lehman would have won. What if his tee-shot on the 16th hadn't hit a TV cameraman's tripod and ricocheted 60 yards back down the fairway? What if it had been propelled forward instead? What if he had holed a 15-foot eagle putt on the 17th, instead of leaving it two inches short of the cup?

Prior to the tournament, Chris DiMarco, who had played his way onto the US team, took Lehman aside. DiMarco told him he had been talking to other players and the general consensus was that, should the captain play his way on to an automatic place on the team by virtue of his performance in the PGA, then he should take it.

But Lehman had already decided that his role at The K Club would be as captain, not as a player. He later explained:

'I decided a while back that, unless there was some crazy, unforeseen circumstance, I would not play … my putting is just a little bit too erratic. I don't putt poorly usually. I don't three putt a lot. I just don't make enough putts, and in the Ryder Cup it's all about the short game, it's all about putting and chipping, is what it comes down to, [and] guys that can knock the ball in the hole.'

Although Lehman brought good form with him into the PGA, it was always more likely that the bigger picture of who would or wouldn't make his US team would prove to be too much of a distraction. As it stood going into the PGA, the top-half of the American team looked exceptionally strong. Tiger Woods and Phil Mickelson, who had each won majors in 2006, and Jim Furyk, who was having one of the best seasons of his career, were all certainties to be on the team. So too were David Toms, Chad Campbell and Chris DiMarco. But the four players occupying the final automatic places were far from safe, and all were 'rookies' as far as the Ryder Cup was concerned.

Vaughn Taylor, JJ Henry, Zach Johnson and Brett Wetterich were hardly household names in their home towns, let alone throughout the United States, yet all had played their way into contention for Ryder Cup debuts. But, with extra points on offer in the PGA Championship, the incentive for players like John Rollins (11th), Stewart Cink (12th), Jerry Kelly (13th), Lucas Glover (14th), Davis Love (15th), Fred Couples (16th), Tim Herron (17th) and Tom Pernice (18th) were enormous. Even Dean Wilson, in 22nd, could dramatically claim a place if he were to follow up his maiden win in the International by also winning in Medinah.

For this final qualifying event for the Ryder Cup, the PGA of America had returned to Medinah, a course in the north-west suburbs of Chicago, which had been lengthened by some 200 yards for this test since the time it last played host to the US PGA Championship in 1999, when Woods had fended off the chasing young Spaniard, Sergio García, over the back nine in the final round.

To be honest, in this age of golf technology, the additional yardage to a golf course didn't intimidate. Modern-day professionals can regularly drive the ball over 300 yards. No, going into the championship, much of the talk in the locker room was more about the substantially changed 17th hole, where the green had been moved closer to the lake, and the seven new greens that course designer Rees Jones had constructed, since he was brought in to alter the course in 2002.

While making the US team or failing to make it occupied the thought processes of many American players heading into the US PGA, one man unconcerned by the possible permutations was Woods. He was already guaranteed to head the US qualifying—

again—and, after his victory in the previous month's British Open, he was the favourite to claim his second major of the season.

Medinah had been the scene of Woods' first PGA triumph in 1999 and, although he had missed nine weeks of the early part of the season due to his father's ill health and subsequent death, Woods had shown an impressive return to form when winning the Open Championship at Hoylake in July and followed up by adding the Buick Open to his list of 'Ws', or wins. On the eve of the PGA, struggling with an allergy, Woods was asked what his continued motivation was. His answer had been emphatic. 'Ws. Just getting Ws. That is why I play; to win; and to beat everybody in the field. That's fun.'

Woods had gone to Medinah on the Monday prior to playing in the Buick Open in Grand Blanc, Michigan. After winning there, a milestone 50th win on the PGA Tour for him, he then returned home to Florida to practice the shots he figured he would require on this latest test, although one aspect of the pre-championship visit left him a bit befuddled. Normally, on returning to courses where he has previously won, Woods likes nothing better than to reminisce and re-enact a particular putt or shot.

When winning the PGA in 1999, Woods felt that the par putt he made on the 17th green in the final round was the critical, deciding factor. Now, it was a different green, a different hole, as he reflected:

'I keep thinking about the putt in the brain, since the green's no longer physically there. I can't go back and hit putts there and reminisce anymore … my life's changed [since 1999] quite a bit, on and off the course. It's a maturation process. I was still very young on tour [then], I didn't really know a lot. I was in my third year and I think it really takes probably a good five years to really and truly understand the tour. I was still young and fresh to the whole thing of being a professional golfer. Things have changed quite a bit since then.'

Woods' words were pretty ominous for any other player aspiring to win the US PGA that week in August, considering that he, more than anyone, had changed and raised the bar for everyone else in the process. Nobody was more aware of this than Sergio García, who had chased him all the way to the line in that 1999 PGA Championship.

But while Woods had gone on to win more and more majors, García came to Medinah seven years on unfulfilled in that particular department. In fact, in a real golfing irony, García had blossomed in the white-heat of Ryder Cup team competition, playing inspiring roles in Europe's wins in 2002 and 2004, but had failed to find the killer instinct necessary to get the job done on the Sunday of a major. Woods, in contrast, had struggled in the team environment.

Now 26 years of age, García would step onto the first tee on his revisit to Medinah for what would be his 32nd major. All he had to do was to reflect on the previous month's British Open, where he started the final round a stroke behind Woods only to finish up seven back, to know that things had not materialised as envisaged. He was the great hope of Europe, the top ranked European in the world rankings, but he had still not managed to win a major. No European had, in fact. Not since Paul Lawrie in the British Open at Carnoustie in 1999.

García was a 'rookie' professional when he played his first PGA Championship in 1999, but he left his mark, in more ways than one, on that tournament. Not only did he chase down Woods, he gave a more physical reminder in the second shot he played from the trunk of a tree on the dogleg 16th. His tee shot had ended up in the right rough, dangerously close to the base of a large red oak tree, in a small indentation between two roots. He had 189 yards to the flag, but rather than chip out, García took a lash at the ball with a six-iron, closing his eyes on impact and risking a wrist injury, and then followed the missile's progress to the green by sprinting on to the fairway and after the ball.

That tree from where García played his second shot on the 16th has become one of the most famous in golf. Since then, countless players have placed a ball in that very spot and tried the shot.

'Everybody and their brother has tried their luck,' said Mike Harrigan, the head club professional at Medinah for 15 years until 2003. 'It was tried 100 times every day for the next year. They were digging a trench out there. Everybody wants to try it, but I don't think anyone can pull it off.'

On the eve of the PGA, García couldn't resist walking over during a practice round to revisit the scene of his greatest, and one of the greatest ever, shots in golf. The next four days of play would determine if he could find inspiration in returning to a favoured place.

•   •   •   •

THERE ARE DIFFERENT TYPES OF pressures to be found on a golf course. As if competing in the US PGA Championship at Medinah didn't have sufficient pressure, for those Europeans (who at least had two more events left), and especially Americans at the last chance saloon, and on the fringes of claiming an automatic Ryder Cup place, the extra stress was palpable.

Davis Love had played in every Ryder Cup match since 1993, the longest active streak by an American. He had started the 2006 season in fourth position on the US Ryder Cup rankings but, by the time he reached Medinah in mid-August, and providing an indication of a disappointing season by his own standards, Love had dropped to 15th in the team rankings. He would require a top eight finish in the PGA if he was to secure an automatic place, otherwise he would have to rely on a pick from Lehman.

Love had suffered a horrible ending to his first round when incurring a triple bogey six on the penultimate hole, and had an equally poor start to his second round with three successive bogeys from the 11th, his second hole. However, the veteran recovered sufficiently to sign for a 69 that left him on 137, seven under, at the midway stage, and believing that the dual aims of the championship and a Ryder Cup place were within his reach. At the mid-point of the championship, he trailed co-leaders Luke Donald, Henrik Stenson, Tim Herron and Billy Andrade by one stroke.

'I've backed myself into a corner [in qualifying for the Ryder Cup] and sometimes you start doing the things you're supposed to be doing a little better when you're backed into a corner,' Love remarked at the tournament.

While Woods lurked with intent on the shoulders of the midway leaders in the championship, the leader board offered much solace to Europe's captain Ian Woosnam. Stenson, whose form had dipped in mid-summer, was already assured of his place on Woosie's team and had also pencilled in a date in December to marry his long-time girlfriend, Emma Lofgren, in what he hoped would be a memorable year. But his immediate goal heading into the weekend at Medinah was to attempt to become the first Swedish male golfer to win a major and to become the first European since Scotland's Tommy Armour in 1930 to annex the PGA title.

Stenson manoeuvred his way to the forefront of the European challenge, and there was some strong back-up, not only from one of his co-leaders, England's Luke Donald, but also Spain's García.

'I'm in a decent position, no doubt about it. But this is a major and it is not easy, no matter what people might think. It's always tough, [but] hopefully I can have a couple more good rounds and see what I can do,' the Spaniard was to observe.

For one man who hadn't made it to Medinah so that he could attend his friend's wife's funeral, his absence hadn't unduly upset his chances of making the European team. Paul McGinley, in the 10th and last automatic place heading down the final stretch of European qualifying, got the news at home that those players in pursuit of him—among them Paul Broadhurst, Johan Edfors, John Bickerton, Kenneth Ferrie and Thomas Bjørn—had all missed the cut.

In Saturday's third round, a semblance of order came about. The air was humid and the greens receptive after heavy overnight rain had doused the course. Tiger Woods stopped lurking and attacked. A course record 65 for 204, 12-under, meant he finished the day in a share of the lead with Luke Donald, who had never been in such a position before. Woods, of course, had. In fact, he was 11 for 0 when carrying the lead or a share of the lead into the final round of majors. As ever, the omens looked to favour him, even if he was to caution: 'There's still a bunch of guys, [who] all have a chance of winning.'

The Woods charge had deflected some of the attention away from the other contest, that of US players attempting to play their way into Lehman's team. Of the surviving contenders, Love was the most disappointed with his third round. On a day when many players took advantage of the benign conditions, Love—despite twice holing out bunker shots for birdies—could only manage a third round 73 that saw him drop from one stroke off the lead at the start of the day down to 18th in the field. Other US hopefuls also struggled. Stewart Cink too shot a third round 73 and Lucas Glover fell out of contention with a 77. Only Tim Herron, it seemed, had left himself with a chance to play his way into the US team going into Sunday's final round.

Taylor, Johnson and Wetterich, the three players occupying the seventh, ninth and 10th positions in the US standings going into the PGA, had all missed the cut and would spend Sunday watching developments at Medinah. As things transpired, it was not to be too anxious a day for any of them as not one of the quartet of

Cink, Glover, Love and Herron, players who each had chances of jumping into automatic places on the final day, could deliver when the tough questions were asked. Herron was the one who had the best chance, but a series of bogeys and a double-bogey saw him fade away to eventually finish in 14th place, a large distance behind the winner Woods.

Just as he did on the parched links of Hoylake in claiming the British Open, he had again mastered all those who conspired to usurp him. This time, on the lush, parkland terrain, he did it with supreme authority, finishing with a final round 68 for 270, 18-under. It was a record-equalling sub-par total in the PGA. He had five shots to spare over runner-up Shaun Micheel, who produced a closing 67 for a season's best finish that left him a stroke clear of the trio—Luke Donald, Sergio García and Adam Scott—who shared third.

As the hands on the large Rolex clock by the first tee moved to 1.50pm, Woods had taken his first stroke in pursuit of his 12th major win. Only Jack Nicklaus, with 18 career majors, has more. Less than ten minutes later, as Woods rolled in a 15-footer for a birdie, just his third stroke of the day, it was to provide him with the outright lead in the championship for the first time, and a lead he was never subsequently to relinquish.

The odds were stacked in Woods' favour as he set out for his final round on a day when a gentle wind caressed the Number 3 course with just enough hint of menace to make players think twice about their club selection and strategy. As a front-runner in golf, he has no peer. In the 39 previous times that he led or shared the 54-hole lead in a tournament, he had won 36 times. In major championships, it was 11 for 11. Now, the statisticians could make that 12 for 12.

Woods produced another master class that condemned all others to a place where they could simply marvel at his deeds. Donald got an up close view of Woods' mastery. In the most extreme test of his career to date, the Englishman was confined to a role of underling, failing to secure a single birdie in a round of 74 to finish on 276.

The world's number one had set out his intent with that birdie on the first hole, and from there on nobody got near to him. When he rolled in a 40-footer for a birdie on the sixth and then holed another raker, from 30 feet, on the eighth, he had moved into a position where the title was his to lose, rather than for others to win. His only bogey, just his third of the entire championship, came on the 17th where his tee-shot finished in a greenside bunker.

But it was immaterial to the outcome by then, so commanding was Woods' play. He had reached the turn in 32, and, message sent, cruised home to yet another championship. It was his third successive win, coming on the back of the British Open and the Buick Open.

That 12th major title moved him into clear second in the all-time list behind Jack Nicklaus' record 18.

'Tiger's a tough guy to beat head-to-head, he just finds a way to win. A lot of people predicted he would give Nicklaus' record a run, but probably not have predicted he would get to 12 this soon [in his career],' was the remark from Furyk. Woods has actually reached the dozen milestone almost three years ahead of Nicklaus.

If anyone was to make any attempt to catch Lehman's attention on that final Sunday, it was runner-up Micheel, who finished alone in second place, a performance that took him from 128th on the US Ryder Cup listings going into the final counting event up to 36th. In his heart, though, Micheel knew it wouldn't be enough to change Lehman's mind.

'I don't expect a call,' Micheel was to explain after finishing his round, and added: 'I was actually lobbying for Davis Love. I talked to Corey Pavin [US vice-captain] on Friday, and I went up to him on the edge of the putting green, and I said, "Look, if you're looking for a guy that's playing really good golf, I'd look towards him [Davis]." In my view, he's swinging about as well as I've seen him swinging. He was playing just great golf.'

The bottom line from Medinah was that Lehman had been left with the very same ten players in his team as had started the week: Tiger Woods, Phil Mickelson, Jim Furyk, Chad Campbell, David Toms, Chris DiMarco, Vaughn Taylor, JJ Henry, Zach Johnson and Brett Wetterich. The status quo had remained, with no change even to the order of qualifying. Lehman would have a night's sleep to decide on the two additional players he would take on the flight from Washington to Dublin.

EIGHT

Eenie, Meanie, Miney, Moe ...

Chicago, United States. August 2006.

TOM LEHMAN WAS UP BRIGHT and early on the morning of Monday, 21 August. But he had not enjoyed a restful night's sleep. All night, he had tossed and turned and wondered which players he should pick as his two 'wild card' selections to complete the United States' 12-man team for the Ryder Cup. He had talked long into the night with his vice-captains, Corey Pavin and Loren Roberts, about his choices, but had not been able to settle on two.

Lehman had gone to bed on the Sunday night at least knowing that Tiger Woods' form was as good as at any time in his career. He had added a comfortable win at Medinah and his victory at the British Open at Hoylake to his amazing record. A number of his other 'big hitters' had also safely come through the qualifying—Phil Mickelson, Jim Furyk, Chad Campbell, David Toms, Chris DiMarco.

Never a man to cast doubt on the ability of any player, Lehman also defended stoutly the fact that the four 'rookies'—Vaughn Taylor, Zach Johnson, JJ Henry and Brett Wetterich—had emerged from the two-year US qualifying system. In his eyes, each one of them had earned the right to be on the flight to Dublin. It was even pointed out that, given the recent history of two successive defeats in the Ryder Cup, at least the newcomers wouldn't have the baggage of knowing what it was like to lose. 'The four guys all earned their spots on this team, qualified through their own good play. They deserve to be there,' he asserted.

Although there had been no change in the ten players who had started the PGA Championship, the last counting tournament in the US qualifying system, from those who finished in automatic places, Lehman still hadn't entirely settled on his two selections and had whittled down a shortlist of six possible picks before he decided to hit the sack and hope that a clearer mind in the morning would help him make his final decision the right one.

The six men on Lehman's shortlist were John Rollins, who had finished 11th in qualifying; Corey Pavin, one of his assistant captains who had played his way into a good run of form, Davis Love, Stewart Cink, Scott Verplank, and Lucas Glover. Rollins and Glover had never played Ryder Cup golf. Selecting either or both would have meant Lehman going into the match with one of the most inexperienced teams in the history of the competition.

'I wasn't married to only picking guys with experience, I was married to picking the two guys who I thought were going to make our team the best team,' Lehman claimed, after announcing that he had opted for experience in Cink, who had placed 12th, and Verplank, who finished 20th in the final US Ryder Cup qualifying table.

The US qualifying system was different from the one employed by the Europeans in that it only rewarded players who secured top-ten finishes in tournaments. Given the number of international players competing on the PGA Tour, this system meant that there were weeks when only one or two Americans claimed points. To counteract this, Lehman had also kept a separate qualifying ranking of his own, based purely on finishes by American players (not just those finishing in the top 10) and Cink was ranked sixth on that list, with Verplank ninth. 'Our guys are clued in, and ready to go,' said Lehman of the match. The last time they had won outside of the United States was at the Belfry in 1993, but he retained his optimism. 'You go down the list and I like them all,' he said.

While the calls to Cink and Verplank brought enthusiastic reactions from the chosen players, Lehman found the other calls difficult to make. But he made them nonetheless, before the official announcement that Cink, who had been a captain's pick by Hal Sutton in 2004, and Verplank, previously a captain's pick by Curtis Strange in 2002, were his preferred choices. In fact, Lehman contacted every one of the players placed between 11th and 25th in the final qualifying table.

Most of the phone calls were made on a Sunday night, after which he had narrowed down the shortlist of six likely lads. He had then decided to sleep on the matter, before making the final decision and the final calls.

Telling Lucas Glover was not a task Lehman enjoyed, as he later explained. 'The call to Lucas may have been the hardest phone call, simply because there's times in your life when you have this gut feeling about somebody and you can't exactly put your finger on what it is and why. You kind of feel like there's something special, and I feel he has that quality ... he was very disappointed, crushed. The thing I can say is, I've been there [passed over for a pick]. I know what it feels like, and it has nothing do with respect or a lack of admiration. It's just that you simply make the two picks you think are best for the team.'

Perhaps the biggest surprise was not who did get a pick, but who didn't. Even though Davis Love had played in every Ryder Cup since 1993, Lehman passed him over for a 'wild card' on the basis that, 'Simply, he hasn't played well, plain and simple. He's been injured ... you know, with all the experience he has and all the things he has accomplished, I still want to have guys who are playing well. I think he has definitely struggled.'

All of which indicated a steeliness in Lehman's psyche, if the truth be known, and that was a trait, everyone agreed, that would be vital if the United States were to end their losing sequence in the Ryder Cup.

Still, neither of Lehman's two wild cards were regular tournament winners. Cink's last tournament win had come in the NEC Invitational in 2004, while Verplank's last win had been back in the 2001 Canadian Open.

'What I'm really wanting, more than anything, is a team that is just tough. Strong guys who will never give up, never quit … our team is unbelievably motivated to win, there's not one guy on the team who is going over there to finish second,' he pointed out.

Cink's 'wild card' pick had been generally anticipated in the Medinah locker room. Verplank's wasn't. But Lehman had been impressed that Verplank had come back from injury intent on gaining a place on the team. 'I don't doubt their heart. Their heart is part of the reason why I picked them.'

Verplank, who had two runner-up finishes early in the season before suffering a shoulder injury, only got back in contention for an automatic place with a tied-fourth finish in the Buick Open two weeks before the PGA, but in the end had to rely on Lehman's wild card for a second Ryder Cup appearance. On hearing of his selection, he showed a lot of enthusiasm.

'To me, there's nothing like going on the road and winning at someone else's house … I think it's such a great event. To me, it's the premiere event in the world. I haven't won a major, maybe one day I will have that chance and get that done. But I don't know how you could be any higher or have a better event than the Ryder Cup. I told Tom I was put on this earth to play in things like this, so I'll be ready to go. I am so fired up.'

· · · ·

Co. Kildare, Ireland. August 2006.

Tiger Woods won his fourth successive tournament when retaining the WGC-Bridgestone Invitational at Akron. He didn't stay around too long to savour this latest success in what was fast becoming a stellar season. Like the other 11 members of the United States team, he made his way to the airport at Cleveland, Ohio, where he boarded a flight chartered by the PGA of America to Dublin, from where the team would make the short inland trip for a flagged reconnaissance visit to The K Club .

It was an appropriate departure point. Cleveland has the reputation for being one of the 'most liveable' cities in the USA. When its Mayor, Frank Jackson, made his inaugural address on assuming office back on 2 January, 2006, he spoke of 'a city of one people, one community, living and working together, with respect, justice and equality.' All of these traits were ones that the US Ryder Cup captain had hoped to instil in his team.

Getting all 12 of his players on the plane to Dublin for a two-day trip was seen as a major coup for Lehman's captaincy. It seemed that he was leaving no stone unturned in getting everyone to bond; players and backroom team. He had picked the brains of some of the top sporting coaches in the USA: John Wooden, Mike Scioscia from the California Angels, Mike Krzyzewski.

On the evening before he named his 'wild card' picks, Lehman had even spent 25 minutes on the phone to Tom Watson. And, all through the qualifying campaign, he had encouraged and cajoled potential team members. His, it seemed, was a captaincy of the age.

Still, this effort showed Lehman's ability to think outside of the box. Although Woods knew the Palmer Course well from his regular pre-British Open golfing and fishing trips to the five-star resort at The Kildare Hotel & Country Club, this was not only a chance for some team-bonding, but also a chance for the other members of the team to get familiar with the course that would stage the Ryder Cup in just less than a month's time.

One accusation traditionally thrown at American teams in the Ryder Cup was that they lacked the same bonding that European teams, despite having players from several different nations, brought to the match. Lehman had never agreed with such an assessment. On the overnight flight from Cleveland, players and caddies mingled. Some played cards. Some slept. Others shot the breeze. It was just what Lehman had hoped for, a show of team spirit.

In the days before the reconnaissance trip took place, Lehman had also been pleased to hear that Woods, demonstrating leadership skills, had taken it on himself to invite the four US team 'rookies' out to dinner at the Diamond Grille restaurant in Akron during the Bridgestone. It was his way of saying to Lehman, 'Don't worry, I'll take care of these guys.'

The US team that got their first sight of The K Club on Monday, 28 August, were in good mood, despite the weather. True to form, the unpredictable Irish weather was the only predictable thing about their first day in Ireland. Which, as far as Lehman was concerned, was exactly what he wanted.

'I'm kind of glad we had this, it's good to see there are several days in a day here in Ireland, where you can get different conditions every half an hour. It's an exercise in patience in many ways.'

Indeed, for Lehman, this was just what the doctor ordered—a hint of the autumnal vagaries that would await his team come the real deal.

'All 12 guys here? It shows a lot of unity,' Stewart Cink, was to remark of the fact that Woods and Phil Mickelson changed business and personal plans made several months previously so that they could make the trip.

Chris DiMarco, too, was impressed with developments. 'I think Tom's done a phenomenal job of getting everyone together

... it says a lot, absolutely, that we're all here. We know who our leaders are on the team and it is nice they are here and they are doing everything we're doing. These guys are here because they are passionate. It wouldn't have been the same without them.'

While team captain Lehman had been given a commitment from ten players that they would definitely be on the plane when he first suggested the two-day bonding session, Woods and Mickelson had to reschedule commitments. Woods, who was due to compete in the Deutsche Bank Championship in Boston that week, had rearranged some duties he was to perform for his Tiger Woods Foundation.

It was, nonetheless, an impressive display of solidarity. Woods, like the rest of the US team, was in relaxed mood, simply looking forward to playing more golf and anticipating keeping his winning streak alive.

'I think you try to keep building each and every week. I have two more tournaments before I come to the Ryder Cup, so hopefully I can play well in those two events,' he commented at the time.

But Woods' record in the Ryder Cup—seven wins, 11 losses and two halved matches prior to The K Club —was contrary to his dominance in individual tournaments. Standing outside the recently expanded Palmer clubhouse with rain testing the quality of his wet suit, Lehman wasn't in any mood to countenance any suggestion that Woods doesn't bring his 'A-Game' to the Ryder Cup, and he stated as much.

'There is nobody in the golfing world, possibly in the sporting world, more committed to winning than him, no matter what the situation. People who question that, don't really understand him at all.'

For his part, Woods, whose only experience of being on a winning Ryder Cup team was at Brookline in 1999, was to comment, 'All you do is try your best, all you can do is to keep grinding, to win points for your team.'

In truth, Lehman couldn't have asked Mother Nature to supply his team with a better preparatory day than the one that presented itself. It was a day of frequently changing weather patterns, one minute sunshine followed the next by heavy showers, and the US team opted to ride in electric carts rather than the more traditional method of walking. For sure, it made for an easier round for the caddies. Lehman opted to play his men in threeballs, so that the four rookies on the team—Zach Johnson, Brett Wetterich, JJ Henry and Vaughn Taylor—could get to know their new teammates.

So it was that Wetterich played with Chad Campbell and David Toms at the head of the field, followed by Taylor with DiMarco and Mickelson, then Johnson with Scott Verplank and Cink, with Henry, Woods and Jim Furyk bringing up the tail. The following day would bring yet more team play, all designed to produce a winning formula for the match that lay ahead.

Lehman, relaxed and eloquent, considered the entire exercise to be a good one. 'I think [the visit] was necessary for all kinds of reasons. A lot of guys had not seen the course, so it was a good thing to do because we want to win, [it] was a day for our four rookie players to go out with the veteran players and see the golf course.'

Lehman, who had previously played the course on a number of occasions in the European Open, felt it was beneficial to see it closer to the tournament. One discovery that the American players made almost immediately was that the greens were playing slower than would be found on the PGA Tour.

Lehman professed to be impressed with the set-up. Although he didn't agree entirely that the strong similarities with US-style courses would give his team any advantage.

'With the quality of players on either side, I don't know if it suits one team more than another. Players on both teams are able to play whatever the course might be and whatever the conditions. You've to drive it well, you've to putt well. It's a tough course.'

Time would only tell if the advance trip had been worth the while.

NINE

Three into Two Doesn't Go!

Munich, Germany. August 2006.

By THE TIME EUROPE'S FINAL qualifying tournament, the BMW International, reached the nondescript course of Eichenried, just north of Munich, team captain Ian Woosnam was in the strong position of being able to pencil seven names onto his team sheet and, so good had their form been throughout the qualifying campaign, he had no worries about including any of them. One by one, the pieces of the jigsaw had fallen into place: Luke Donald, Sergio García, Henrik Stenson, David Howell, Colin Montgomerie, Robert Karlsson and Paul Casey.

No matter what happened on the flat, parkland course with overhead power cables crisscrossing its terrain during the BMW, nothing—barring some supernatural force—could have displaced any of the septet who had each qualified so impressively. Padraig Harrington, too, had looked to be a safer bet to take his place in the automatic ten, requiring as it would a bizarre sequence of circumstances if he were to be deprived.

In truth, Woosnam couldn't have asked for much more from the previous twelve months of qualifying, a process that had started with the Omega European Masters in Crans, Switzerland, the previous September. There, García and Donald had immediately put down their Ryder Cup intentions by finishing first and second, to get off to fast starts in their respective attempts at securing automatic places. García, based mainly on the PGA Tour, had required a 'wild card' at The Belfry in 2002 and Donald had needed one for the 2004 match in Detroit.

Perhaps Woosnam would have wanted Lee Westwood, or Thomas Bjørn, or Darren Clarke, or Ian Poulter—or even the US-based Swede Carl Petterson, who had won twice on the PGA Tour inside a year—to play their way into the team. But that would have been greedy in the extreme, and the reserve list of players simply acted to confirm the ever-growing strength in depth on the PGA European Tour. It was all a far cry from the days in the 1960s and 1970s when the United States regularly outclassed their opponents from Great Britain and Ireland, a time when Jack Nicklaus suggested enough was enough and that the parameters should be widened to embrace an all-European team rather than one representing the two islands on the periphery of the continent.

The reality was that Woosnam could have had few complaints from a dual system of qualifying that, firstly, took five players from a table based on world points accumulated at counting tournaments and, then, secondly, completed the automatic ten places available from points earned on a European points list.

In the main, the jostling for qualifying spots had lacked much of the drama or the constant changing of positions of previous campaigns. England's Paul Broadhurst, whose one and only Ryder Cup appearance was in the 1991 match at Kiawah Island, a match given the label of the 'War on the Shore' so jingoistic had been the atmosphere at a time of the Gulf War, showed good early-season form to move into automatic contention after his second place finish in the Wales Open. He had previously won the Portuguese Open and was second in the Qatar Masters. But, whether the anxiety of Ryder Cup qualifying got to him or if it was just down to losing form, Broadhurst missed the cut in six of his next nine tournaments and went to Munich basically needing to win or finish second to have had any chance of qualifying for the team.

John Bickerton had played his way briefly onto the team when winning the French Open in early July but the Englishman stumbled over the summer months in his quest for a first-ever Ryder Cup appearance, missing the cut at the European Open, Scottish Open and the US PGA in three of his next four tournaments. His best finish in the run-in to qualifying had been a tied-48th finish in the Open Championship at Hoylake and, like Broadhurst, he had gone to the BMW International needing to win.

The real surprise package of the season on the European Tour in 2006 was unquestionably Johan Edfors, the Swede who had only earned his tour card through the secondary Challenge Tour in 2005. Edfors had failed to retain his card in his maiden season on the full tour in 2004 but made a massive impact at the second time of asking when winning three tournaments—the TCL Classic in China, the Quinn Direct British Masters and the Barclays Scottish Open—and had arrived in Munich knowing that nothing less than a victory or a runner-up finish would enable him to gatecrash his way onto the team.

The two players most precariously placed in the qualifying table going were José María Olazábal, who had decided not to play in Munich and instead went shooting, and Paul McGinley. McGinley was tenth and last in the composite rankings. But things were not quite as straightforward, as Olazábal, fifth on the world points list, held only a miniscule advantage over Montgomerie, and would fall back behind McGinley on the European points table if the Scot finished tied-47th or better in the final counting tournament.

Olazábal decided he was too tired to travel, taking the gamble that he was still far enough ahead of 11th placed Broadhurst on the European points list, and his absence from the BMW tournament came as a shock to many of his fellow players. The Spaniard hadn't played in the Ryder Cup since the 1999 match at Oakland Hills and it was felt by his peers that he was taking an unnecessary risk in staying away, with the likes of Edfors, Broadhurst and Bickerton all capable of bypassing him in the table.

'I'd be here [if in the same position], that's all I would say. I mean, all he has to do is turn up and beat Monty this week to be guaranteed his place. But he has definitely done myself and Paul no harm at all,' observed Harrington on the eve of the tournament.

Montgomerie was more to the point. 'I was surprised when I heard Olazábal was not playing. After a full year of trying to qualify and then to say you are tired, I'm very surprised. There is a long winter ahead to be tired,' said Monty, who also wasn't immune from doing a strange thing himself during the tournament when making a trip home to Scotland. On the Saturday evening, after completing his third round, Montgomerie travelled with the Ryder Cup trophy in his jet to attend a Robbie Williams concert in Glasgow, before returning back to Germany to complete his final round.

After a qualifying campaign that had lasted the best part of a year, the final euro and cents were totted up at the conclusion of the BMW with Woosie charged with the task of adding his two 'wild card' picks. The Welshman appeared nervous in the run-up to the final tournament. For much of the year, he had been readily available for interviews in the week of a tournament but, in Munich, he was reluctant to talk to media who had travelled from all over Europe and had to be persuaded by a tour official to give the standard interview.

On the previous Monday, the entire US team, led by Lehman, had made a reconnaissance trip to play the Palmer Course, and there was a sense that Lehman was doing everything right in his captaincy. It had also been revealed that Lehman had even been in contact with the previous European captain, Bernhard Langer. Woosnam had stubbornly refused to pick Langer's brain, preferring instead to confide in his close friend Sam Torrance and learn from his own experiences in the team room as a player.

When finally put under the microscope before the final event in the build-up to the Ryder Cup, Woosnam refused to talk about specific players.

'There's a queue of players who are on my list to qualify or be picked, [and] I'm not going to talk about any player individually because I think it's very unfair,' he remarked, and then added: 'I think it's going to be one of the hardest things I've ever had to do. I've a lot of good friends out there who are desperate to be on the team. I've got to pick the two players who I think are going to be strongest for the team.'

What did transpire at the eve of tournament interview was that Darren Clarke, who hadn't played since the British Open in July, had made himself available for a captain's pick. The Northern Irishman had also signalled his intentions to play before the Ryder Cup by entering the Madrid Open, the week beforehand.

Left unsaid, but probably providing a more meaningful indicator of a pick, was Lee Westwood's inclusion in the tournament. Although the English player didn't play in the pro-am, Westwood, who had been battling illness since the Bridgestone in Akron the previous week, got out of his sick bed to play after Woosnam pleaded with him.

· · · ·

WHEN PADRAIG HARRINGTON, WHO HAD celebrated his 35th birthday the previous day, shook hands with his friend McGinley at the conclusion of the second round, his mood was far more upbeat than that of his fellow Dubliner. Harrington had played his way into contention in the tournament with two good opening rounds, but his first actions, however, were to congratulate McGinley— with whom he had won a World Cup of Golf in 1997 and shared so much of his golfing life—on making the team.

'It's been nine months with a noose around his neck and it's been nine months of hell for him and the best thing that can happen to Paul is that it's finished. It's over and done with and now he can get on with things,' Harrington observed, in assessing that McGinley's qualifying campaign had finally come to a successful end.

Harrington's early congratulations to McGinley were issued as much on the basis of good play from Montgomerie, who was certain to overtake Olazábal in the world points list and thereby lessening the chances of anyone overtaking McGinley on the second European table, as on McGinley's own form which had shown no sign of improvement over the first two rounds of the International. He was to be proven right. McGinley's poor form had continued and he had missed the cut in Munich. But so too had John Bickerton. And, although Paul Broadhurst and Johan Edfors survived into the weekend, they would not contend for the title and were eventually to finish in tied-59th and tied-68th positions respectively.

Just as the American qualifying campaign had concluded at the PGA Championship in Medinah with the same ten players who had started the event claiming the automatic places in Tom Lehman's team, neither were there any significant changes to the standings to the ten automatic places on the European team after Munich. The only difference was that Olazábal dropped from the world points list to the European points list, taking the tenth and final position.

Woosnam had walked around the course all week as if the weight of the world was on his shoulders, but he should have been heartened by the final result which confirmed the well-being of so many of his players. Henrik Stenson won the tournament. Harrington was one of those —along with the South African Retief Goosen—who was beaten in a play-off by the Swede, to finish in second place for the third time in 2006. David Howell claimed fourth position, and Luke Donald and Colin Montgomerie shared sixth.

· · · ·

WHEN WOOSNAM WALKED INTO THE media centre on Sunday evening, 3 September, to officially announce his captain's selections, the bounce in his step was not as light as might have been envisaged after such a strong showing by so many of his team. He still wore the look of a troubled man. The reason was Denmark's Thomas Bjørn.

Up to the end, Bjørn, who had failed to make the team in 2004, his only involvement being his acting as a lieutenant to captain Bernhard Langer, had hoped against hope that he would somehow earn Woosnam's approval. He didn't. Neither did Carl Petterson, nor Ian Poulter. Darren Clarke and Lee Westwood were the two players chosen by Woosnam to complete the team.

Clarke's inclusion to play, so shortly after his wife's death, brought a round of applause in the media centre where Woosnam delivered his two picks. The clapping seemed to soothe Woosnam's fears. Europe's captain revealed that he had extended the invite to Clarke the previous Thursday, the first day of the BMW, and that the Ulsterman had accepted.

'I don't think it is a risk at all … believe me, Darren is up for it. It's going to be a very emotional time for Darren, [but] with all the guys and all the families and all the players, it will be like one big family for him. I'm sure Darren is going to cope very fine. He won't be thinking about anything but the Ryder Cup and winning,' insisted Woosnam.

Westwood's inclusion was more of a last-minute affair. Not long before Woosnam had arrived in to the media centre to name his two picks, Bjørn had been seen leaving the clubhouse with a smile on his face. Some cute observer had put two and two together and come up with five. Nobody ever discovered the reason for Bjørn's smile, because he was not Woosnam's second choice. Like Clarke, Westwood had previously won the European Open over the Palmer Course but Woosnam only decided on him as a second pick, ahead of Bjørn, less than an hour before he made his announcement public.

Critically, again pointing to the contrast in captaincy, Woosnam had not informed Bjørn that he would not be picked. Neither had he told Westwood, who was already airborne with his mobile phone switched off, before Woosnam—after consultation with his vice-captains Peter Baker and Des Smyth—finally made his decision and attempted to call him. Westwood got the news he'd hoped for only on arrival back in England.

'He's won twice around The K Club and I think that made a difference,' said Woosnam of his decision to go with Westwood, then ranked 47th in the world, ahead of Bjørn, a player ranked 35th. 'I feel for the guys who haven't made the team, and I've got to say how strong European golf is at the moment that we have so many great players … but I have to go with my gut feeling,' he explained.

It should have been a proud night for Woosnam. Instead, he was subjected to questions querying his manner of captaincy. While Lehman had organised regular team gatherings, including a full team bonding session at The K Club, and wrote personal letters earlier in the year to all potential members of his team, setting out what he expected from them if the United States were to regain a trophy they hadn't held since 1999, Woosnam's first team get-together wouldn't take place until the Monday before the actual match.

The reason why Europe hadn't performed similar bonding sessions to the Americans, according to Woosnam, was due to travel logistics. 'Some guys are playing in different countries and it is difficult to get them all together,' he explained.

. . . .

Thomas Bjørn had left Golfclub München Nord-Eichenried in a BMW courtesy car with no word from Woosnam on whether he would be a captain's pick. Working on the basis that 'no news is good news,' Bjørn—a two-time Ryder Cup player at Valderrama in Spain in 1997 and the Belfry in England in 2002—returned to his hotel room in the centre of Munich where he switched on his television set and watched Woosie's press conference. He didn't like what he heard.

Bjørn wasn't surprised that one pick had gone to Clarke. But he was devastated that he had been passed over for the second pick without even a word in the ear from Woosnam.

'Let me say from the outset that I have nothing against Lee Westwood. Lee is a fantastic golfer, a great guy … but if you can find one category in which he has beaten me, then I would like to see it. Woosnam has got nothing to base his decision on,' said Bjørn soon after the news reached him.

He continued: 'Earlier this year, Woosnam warned players to be careful if they were playing a lot in the United States, saying he was going to pick players who based themselves in Europe. Then he picks Lee, who spent most of the first half of the year in America. If he had picked [Carl] Petterson I wouldn't have had a problem, because he has won twice in America. How can you argue with the way Carl has played this year? With all due respect to Lee, he has not been playing well, he hasn't won this year, and he hasn't been at the top of his game.

'This will be the first time I don't even watch the Ryder Cup on television, and you don't know how sad that is, given how much I care for the tournament, the European Tour and the competition itself. I desperately want the 12 players to be a success, but I want them to do it in spite of the captain. There are a lot of people feeling uneasy about the Woosie captaincy. Stories will start to come out ... I have had a lot of things to deal with in my career but this is the hardest.

'This is harder even than what happened at the [British] Open in 2003 [when he suffered a late final round collapse, allowing Ben Curtis to win] and The K Club [in 2005, when he took an 11 on the 17th in the final round of the European Open.] Everywhere I went after those occasions, people told me that I had to get back on the horse. But here, I am just completely lost for words. Of course I will have to pick myself up, but it is going to be difficult.'

When Woosnam eventually got around to talking with Bjørn on the Sunday night, the conversation was short and not too sweet.

'He wasn't a happy chappy,' admitted the European captain. 'He was very, very disappointed. He didn't say a lot. I tried to say, "I hope you respect my decision." But someone has got to do the job. Someone's got to pick the team. I feel sorry for the guys who've missed out. Hopefully, when this blows over, after a while, we can have a few beers over it.'

Bjørn's outburst against Woosnam came at a price, a hefty fine from the PGA European Tour. He was forced to issue an apology to Woosnam. But Bjørn had made his point. The more serious concern for Woosnam was whether it would lead to any disharmony in the camp.

TEN

'If'

Co. Kildare, Ireland. Monday, 18 September, 2006.

THE FIRST CHINK IN THE armour of Tom Lehman's captaincy came
on the day his plane out of Washington, DC, finally touched
down in a rainy Dublin. It was a little over three hours behind
schedule. Admittedly the late arrival wasn't Lehman's fault. While a
technical glitch was the logical explanation for the delay, Lehman's
version centred around the fact that his team had packed too
many suitcases for a trip that, for most of them, extended into the
following week's WGC-American Express Championship at The
Grove, outside London.

Clothes, for on and off the course, were not the sole reason for
the luggage overload. It transpired that Team USA had decided
that one of the key requirements for their stay in Ireland was to
bring sufficient quantities of tortilla chips to keep the team suitably
nourished while housed in the West Wing of the five-star hotel at
The K Club. Melissa Lehman, the captain's wife, had sourced the
chips and also packed ingredients to make home-made salsa.

Prior to the team's departure, a rather more serious note had
been struck when the American players attended the Walter Reed
Hospital in Washington to visit US soldiers who had been injured
in combat in Iraq and Afghanistan. Lehman had first made the
trip alone during the Booz Allen tournament in 2005 and decided

that it would be a good idea to bring the official party back to the hospital.

When in the hospital, Lehman's players had listened to a young soldier recall the horror of how he had been shot while travelling in a tank and had to be transferred to another one in order to get back to safety, only for the second vehicle to also get struck by a mortar. It exploded into flames, and the medics with the soldier started to panic because they weren't used to being in such a situation.

'The kid who had been shot had to talk down the medic, to open the hatch,' recalled Lehman. They had only just escaped from the vehicle when it incinerated. 'It was just a bunch of melted metal when it was all done,' was how the solider put it to the US captain.

Lehman later insisted the visit to the military hospital was 'Not to find any special recipe for our Ryder Cup team, we went there because it was the right thing to do as Americans and [to] support our troops.'

Tiger Woods, Phil Mickelson and Jim Furyk, the top three players in the world rankings, and seen as the vital elements in the team if the United States were to avoid an unprecedented third successive defeat, weren't a part of the official visiting party to the injured soldiers. Woods and Furyk were already on the other side of the Atlantic, where they had been first round losers in the HSBC World Matchplay at Wentworth, and Mickelson had attended his sister's wedding and met up with the team in Dublin.

Woods, who had won five successive strokeplay tournaments prior to heading to Wentworth, showed how relaxed he was ahead of the match by taking in an English FA Premiership match at Chelsea's home ground, Stamford Bridge, on the Sunday, where he saw Didier Drogba score an extraordinary goal to seal victory for his team.

After his matchplay loss, demonstrating his intent to be a mainstay of the US team, Furyk, along with his caddie Fluff

Cowan, had decided it would be a good thing to head over to The K Club early to get more familiarised with the course. He was the only player to get in a practice round on the Sunday, which, ironically, he managed to do in bright sunshine and with only a gentle breeze. For the rest of the week, players were forced to contend with the tail-end of a hurricane that swept in from the mid-Atlantic, bringing with it strong winds and heavy rain.

Lehman and the nine players who travelled over from Washington had been met on the tarmac at the airport in Dublin by Ian Woosnam. The team had arrived at Dublin Airport and disembarked wearing an outfit suspiciously like that of Irish tweed. It was, in actual fact, Ralph Lauren. Lehman described it as, 'The Great Gatsby look … earth tones. It has some depth to it, and has some history, tradition, which I like.'

The two captains shook hands firmly and warmly. It was obvious that each was glad that the build-up was nearly over, that the time for competition was nigh.

Lehman had assumed the US captaincy on 11 November, 2004. The 24th man to take on the role as captain, Lehman's task differed from that of the captains before him in one crucial aspect: none of his predecessors had ever been asked to take charge of a team attempting to avoid a third straight defeat. At the time of his appointment, Lehman, a three-time Ryder Cup player and the PGA Tour's Player of the Year in 1996 when he won the British Open, had remarked: 'Sometimes you never dream big enough.'

With the two-year qualifying campaign completed and, it seemed, one of the most bonded American teams of recent years, Lehman's mood on arrival at the venue was, as usual, good humoured.

Woosnam had been billeted at The K Club for a number of days ahead of Team USA's arrival. When he announced his two 'wild card' picks in Munich a fortnight earlier, the Welshman had seemed ill at ease and uncomfortable. But the time spent away from the glare of publicity and the fact that all the decisions had been taken seemed to bring with it greater confidence.

If Lehman was a traditionalist in terms of clothing, Woosie was more of a traditionalist in the team concept, of getting the players into the team room and doing much of his cajoling and bonding behind closed doors. 'You know, a lot of things happen in the team room. The guys have to perform on the golf course but a lot goes on in the team room [for a player] to go out and enjoy it. If you don't enjoy it, it's hard work,' he explained.

Those members of his team who had not made their own way to Dublin arrived on a flight from Heathrow a number of hours after the Americans. Woosnam met the remainder of his team, and then, just like any Dublin motorist, had to contend with the nightmare traffic on the M50 motorway to get to The K Club for the start of the serious business of preparing his team for the defence of the Ryder Cup.

The first surprise of Lehman's opening media conference was that he admitted to already knowing which players would comprise his four four-balls come Friday morning. 'The four teams, do I know them? I do.'

'Since when?' he was asked.

'I would say within the last couple of weeks,' he admitted. But he refused to add to the intrigue by actually naming the eight players.

Instead, he played a game. Lehman explained: 'Let me give you a "what if?" What would you do if you put four teams out every day that kept on winning? Would you split up a winning team in that scenario? What happens to the rest of the guys? I wouldn't prefer not to play everybody [in the fourballs and foursomes]. I don't think it would be the wisest, come singles time, not to play everybody. But what do you do if something like that happens? We're here to win, and if things are going great, then we all just, you know, take one for the team.'

Whether he knew his fourball pairings at that stage isn't clear, but Woosnam refused to follow Lehman's lead. He made it clear he would watch each and every player in practice before committing to any formations, as he pointed out.

'We've got 12 great players this year, probably the strongest team we've ever had. They are all prepared to play with whoever they want to play with, it's up to me to get the pairings right … there's so many different pairings I can use. I'll see how everybody is performing before I actually put out my pairings.'

Woosnam, more than anyone, was glad that the phoney war was over. 'Yeah, 18 months ago I was nominated as captain. It seemed to take a long time to get here, but the last few weeks have gone really quick. I'm just looking forward to it. The team is looking forward to it.'

The Thomas Bjørn incident, as far as Woosnam was concerned, was a thing of the past.

Darren Clarke was one of those who had received a 'wild card' from Woosnam. The week after getting that call-up, Clarke had joined five other members of the European team in a surreptitious visit to Straffan that was quite unlike the much-publicised exercise conducted some weeks previously by the Americans.

Clarke played a round of golf with Luke Donald, Paul Casey, José María Olazábal, David Howell and Padraig Harrington and, then, the following week had returned to tournament play in the Madrid Open. He wanted to play Madrid for two reasons: firstly, to get back some tournament sharpness; secondly, to get all of the media requirements out of the way so that he could focus on golf once he got to the Ryder Cup.

Clarke had sat in the small media centre at the La Moraleja club in Madrid on the eve of the tournament and bared his soul. He spoke for 22 minutes of personal heartache, of his decision to play.

'It was pretty obvious from early on in the season that if I was going to play, I was going to have to be a pick. I was trying to play as well as I could on the few occasions that I did so I could show Woosie that I was playing well,' he said.

After Heather's death, which came at the end of a five year long battle with cancer, the recurrence of the disease being diagnosed two weeks after the 2004 Ryder Cup, Clarke said he faced 'a very tough decision' on whether to make himself available to play.

'I know Heather would have wanted me to play. I would have missed it if I didn't think I could contribute,' he said. The fact he'd played well in past Ryder Cups, that it was in Ireland and that it was matchplay made up his mind.

Most of all, Clarke insisted, he was playing because that would have been his wife's wish. 'She was always very much behind me, pushing me out there, kicking me out the door to go and play tournaments. She wasn't the sort of person who would want me to sit around and mope at home. She would want me out there working, as long as the boys were okay. I don't know if it is a release [on the golf course] or not, but it's me getting back to normality, getting back to my way of life and what I did before. Life has changed now and my priorities are my kids ... at some stage, I have to grow up. This is the prime time for it. I have added responsibilities now and I have to do the right thing, both by my boys and my job.'

Clarke didn't win in Madrid. He finished tied-31st in a week where Ian Poulter, one of those passed over for a captain's pick, claimed victory. But his performance gave him the reassurance he needed that he was up to the task of playing a Ryder Cup. On his arrival at the Palmer Course at the start of Ryder Cup week, he explained:

'I was desperate to be here. But, at the same time, if I didn't think I could contribute to the team and be a benefit to the team, I would have made the decision to not be available to play.'

On that Monday night when Team Europe adjourned to their team room in the East Wing of the hotel, it had been to view a motivational video of past heroic golfing deeds, to the accompaniment of Rudyard Kipling's poem, 'If':

'If you can keep your head when all about you
Are losing theirs and blaming it on you …
If you can meet with Triumph and Disaster,
And treat those two impostors just the same …'

As far as Woosnam was concerned, the time to get serious, for Clarke and the rest of the team, had come. Rather than leave the video until later in the week, Woosnam decided that it would be better for them to get into the right team spirit from the word go. It was to be the sort of wise decision making that became a feature of his captaincy.

The motivational video had become an integral part of European preparations in the times that Woosnam had played in the Ryder Cup. The video for 2006 was put together for Woosnam by TWI and Kipling's words were narrated by Tony Adamson, a former golf correspondent with BBC Radio. Woosnam had first viewed it a number of weeks ahead of the Ryder Cup, and he was instantly smitten by what he saw. When the players watched and listened, they were too. They went to bed knowing what feats they would be required to emulate to become the first European side in history to win a third straight Ryder Cup.

There was no motivational video for the American team, who decided that their first night in Ireland should be devoted to a barbecue and a sing-song, led by Chad Campbell's wife, Amy, who had once considered a career as a professional singer. The tortillas, apparently, stayed in their containers. Uneaten.

Thomas Bjørn didn't make the 2006 Ryder Cup team and was bitterly disappointed not to be one of the captain's 'wild card' picks. He predicted that Ian Woosnam's captaincy wouldn't be a success, but was soon proved wrong as Woosnam led Europe to victory. © *Matt Browne / Sportsfile*

Former US President, George Bush Senior was one of the celebrity visitors to the K Club. Another former US President who attended the 2006 Ryder Cup was Bill Clinton. © *David Maher / Sportsfile*

Lee Westwood chips from the bunker on the
third during the first day of practice ahead of
the 36th Ryder Cup Matches. © *David Maher /
Sportsfile*

Above: Padraig Harrington drives from the 5th during the first day of practice.
© *David Maher / Sportsfile*

Below: Elin Woods, wife of Tiger Woods, during the formal opening ceremony on the 21st September.
© *Brendan Moran / Sportsfile*

JJ Henry plays his second shot from the fairway on the 17th hole during Friday morning's fourball matches.
© *Damien Eagers / Sportsfile*

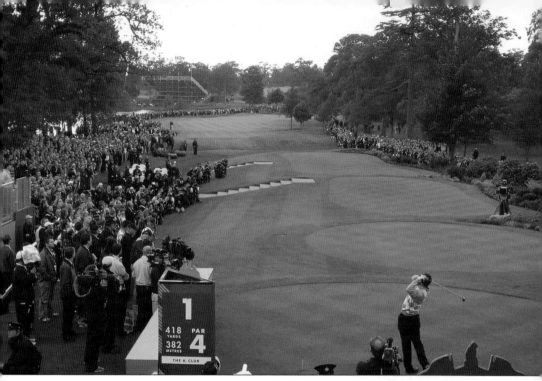

Above: Tiger Woods tees off from the first tee box during Friday morning's four-ball matches. © *David Maher / Sportsfile*

Below: Tiger checks his lie before taking a free drop during the same game. © *Brendan Moran / Sportsfile*

Paul McGinley reacts after missing a putt on the 16th green during Friday afternoon's foursomes matches. © *David Maher / Sportsfile*

Right: Zach Johnson celebrates after holing a putt on the 15th green during Saturday morning's four-ball matches. © *Damien Eagers / Sportsfile*

Below: José María Olazábal, left, is congratulated by playing partner Sergio García during Saturday morning's four-ball matches. © *David Maher / Sportsfile*

Above: JJ Henry reacts after a missed putt on the 18th green, which would have won the match for the USA during Saturday morning's four-ball matches. © *Brendan Moran / Sportsfile*

Right: Darren Clarke is congratulated by Tiger Woods after his birdie chip at the 16th hole for victory over Woods/ Furyk during Saturday morning's four-ball matches. © *Matt Browne / Sportsfile*

Above: Paul Casey lines up a putt on the fourth green during Saturday morning's four-ball matches. © *Brendan Moran / Sportsfile*

Right: Casey is congratulated by playing partner David Howell after Casey got a hole in one on the 14th during Saturday afternoon's foursomes matches. © *Matt Browne / Sportsfile*

Above: Jim Furyk watches his drive on the 15th during Saturday morning's four-ball matches while Tom Lehman (inset), Team USA captain, observes the action. © *Matt Browne / Sportsfile*

Below: Team Europe playing partners, Padraig Harrington and Paul McGinley with Tiger Woods during Saturday afternoon's foursomes matches. © *David Maher / Sportsfile*

Left: Colin Montgomerie lines up a putt on the 18th green during Saturday afternoon's foursome matches. © *Damien Eagers / Sportsfile*

Below: European captain, Ian Woosnam, congratulates Darren Clarke on his win over Zach Johnson on Sunday afternoon. © *David Maher / Sportsfile*

Above: Darren Clarke celebrating with Henrik Stenson, whose 4 and 3 win over Vaughn Taylor on Sunday was the moment that Europe were guaranteed victory in the 2006 Ryder Cup© *Damien Eagers / Sportsfile*

Below: Sergio García celebrates Team Europe's victory with the crowd. © *Matt Browne / Sportsfile*

Above: Team Europe with the Ryder Cup after winning it for the third time in a row. Back row (l-r): Lee Westwood, Darren Clarke, Padraig Harrington, Henrik Stenson, Robert Karlsson, David Howell, Colin Montgomerie.
Front row (l-r): José María Olazábal, Paul McGinley, Ian Woosnam, Sergio García, Luke Donald, Paul Casey. © *David Maher / Sportsfile*

Below: Irish members of Team Europe—Darren Clarke, Paul McGinley and Padraig Harrington show their true colours. © *David Maher / Sportsfile*

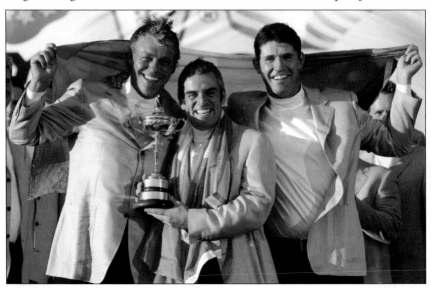

ELEVEN

One Million Reasons ...

Co. Kildare, Ireland. Tuesday, 19 September, 2006.

THE FIRST REAL INDICATION THAT the Ian Woosnam who turned up as captain at The K Club was different from the one who had seemingly been outmanoeuvred by Tom Lehman in the months running up to the event, came just before lunchtime on the first day of official practice. The previous day had been a settling in affair for the two teams, in many ways the calm before the storm, with the meteorologists only starting to keep track of the easterly moving Hurricane Gordon that had just hit the Azores in the mid-Atlantic.

From early morning of that first practice day, the crowds—numbering 45,000 for practice and tournament days—had moved through the intricate security measures at the entrance gates to The K Club and found places on grandstands behind tees and greens, on slippery and grassy slopes, or had congregated in one of the public areas. The event organisers, having learnt from the Irish Open at nearby Carton House, where heavy rain had caused inconvenience for golf fans in May, made sure these were decked out extensively with wooden flooring to counteract whatever the weather gods attempted to throw at the host venue.

Even on practice days, players, or captains, didn't have to do much to earn applause from spectators. And, so, when Woosnam walked onto the ninth green just after midday, it was to a rich round of applause from those gathered on the grassy mounds that ran around the green. Woosnam acknowledged the applause only briefly, with a single wave of his hand, his mind on more serious matters. Word had come back to him that Darren Clarke and David Howell had left balls in the bunkers early on in their practice rounds and Woosnam was determined that such a situation wouldn't arise in the actual competition.

The overnight rain, in excess of one and a quarter inches, had changed the texture of the sand in the bunkers, with the result that Clarke and Howell had failed to properly execute shots. Woosnam felt that the fault lay with how the bunkers had been raked.

'You just can't get out of them, there's so many rake marks,' remarked Woosnam, who took matters into his own hands by physically taking rakes from the green staff and demonstrating how it should be done. He wanted all of the bunkers raked with grooves running towards the green, and took his task so seriously that he tried four different types of rakes before settling on one. 'At least if the ball is lying in a groove mark, you're going with the groove rather than against it. That's how I'd like to see it,' he explained.

Woosnam's hands-on approach was more to his liking than the necessary evil of public speaking or the task of sitting behind a microphone and explaining his thoughts to a ravenous media who had travelled in strength from all over Europe and the United States. He had handpicked his back-up two vice-captains, Peter Baker and Des Smyth, players he had soldiered with on tour when the pickings were lean, and, once immersed in the team environment, Woosie had increasingly gained the respect of his players. The foreboding that had been predicted by Thomas Bjørn seemed misplaced.

On that first official day of practice, Woosnam—who went more with geographical ties than any overt game plan—had seemed less inclined to show his hand than his opposite number

Tom Lehman, who blatantly paired Tiger Woods with Jim Furyk and Chris DiMarco with Phil Mickelson.

DiMarco had impressed Lehman, who extolled his virtues. 'He's a great team-mate, phenomenal. He's everyone's friend, everyone's buddy. But his passion is what he brings to the team room. He loves football, loves the Florida Gators. He loves his wife, kids, his friends. He loves the Ryder Cup. I don't think there is a tournament in the world he'd rather participate in and win more.'

When Europe had inflicted the heaviest ever defeat on the United States in the match at Oakland Hills, DiMarco stood at the back of the 18th green and forced himself to watch the celebrations. He wanted to imprint the desolation of defeat so that it could be unwrapped for the next time, driving him to avoid a repetition. 'It was the fact that we got our butts handed to us and there they were celebrating on our green,' he recalled.

The Americans had headed out early for their first day's practice, but not as early as had been the case at The Belfry in 2002, when Woods had virtually completed his practice rounds before the spectators had been allowed through the gates. At Straffan, Woods adhered to playing to the agreed team times, which at least gave attendees on the practice days an opportunity to catch the world's number one in action.

Those early arrivals for the first practice day would have seen an utterly relaxed Woods. At one point in their game, Brett Wetterich made a 15-footer for birdie on the 11th hole and went to high-five Woods. Woods' response was to jokingly shove Wetterich away.

It wasn't a sign of disrespect, more that Woods was comfortable in the rookie's company. He was more of a team player, more at home, than at any previous Ryder Cup.

To anyone observing that first practice session, it was obvious that Woods would play alongside Furyk, just as they had done at the 2005 President's Cup. Furyk had become Woods' foil in team competition. He'd heard the old jokes in the American team locker room at past Ryder Cups that involved US captains passing around sheets of paper asking players who they'd like to play with, but also who they would be uncomfortable playing with.

'We always joked that we had 11 guys that had "Tiger Woods" written on the [uncomfortable] sheet ... maybe some people are intimidated,' said Furyk.

Perhaps the weight of letting Woods down with some poor shots had a detrimental effect on some of his old partners. But, in Furyk, Woods had found an unlikely kindred spirit. The partnership was forged in securing the President's Cup in Canada the previous year, where they secured two and a half from three points, and continued—albeit with not quite the same success level—at the Ryder Cup.

In attempting to work out why there should be chemistry between himself and Tiger, Furyk explained: 'Our mentalities are a lot the same. We attack a lot of holes in similar ways. We read putts very similarly. Our thought processes are a lot alike. Obviously, he can attack the golf course from different angles than I can because of his power and length, but that helps in fourball type competition ... you know, we get along pretty well.

'Tiger's the best player in the world, so you want to put him in positions where he can take advantage and play his game and play well.'

One thing that Furyk had on his side as he headed into the Ryder Cup was form. Apart from a first round exit in the previous week's World Matchplay, his form in the run-up to the match had been mightily impressive, surpassed only by one man: Woods! Furyk had gone 2nd-4th-4th-2nd-29th-3rd-1st in the seven tournaments running from the US Open in Winged Foot up to winning the Canadian Open a fortnight before the Ryder Cup.

'We're all excited to get these [practice] days under our belt and it is good preparation, [but] everyone's excited for Friday,' he said.

Woods had long since finished playing with Furyk, Wetterich and Scott Verplank, and was practising alone at the far end of the driving range when he was spied by Darren Clarke, who, having walked off the ninth green in his money match with Lee Westwood against Padraig Harrington and Paul McGinley, had spent a considerable amount of time signing autographs.

Clarke took a diversion to the 10th tee after spotting Woods, breaking away from his intended route to finally meet his friend in the flesh for the first time since his wife had died. Woods threw his arms around Clarke in a bear hug that drew polite applause from those who had gathered in the grandstand behind the range, the crowd reacting almost as if embarrassed to be peeping in on a personal occasion. That night, the seating plans at the teams' cocktail dinner were arranged so that Clarke and Woods sat beside each other.

At that dinner, Paul Casey came in for a tough old time from his team-mates. He had arrived on the official team flight from Heathrow having claimed the £1 million top prize at the World Matchplay, where he had beaten American Shaun Micheel in a one-sided final. Colin Montgomerie, who had undergone a publicised divorce settlement with his ex-wife Eimear earlier in the year, was one of those who gently inquired as to Casey's financial well being at the dinner.

'Monty was giving me a hard time, asking if I wanted to swap bank accounts. I declined,' joked Casey afterwards.

What impressed Woosnam most about Casey, though, had been the Englishman's assertion that he would rather win the Ryder Cup than collect the million pound cheque at the World Matchplay. To Woosnam, that said more than a million words about the kind of team spirit that had been instilled into his European team in the run-up to the actual competition.

TWELVE

Tiger Attack

Co. Kildare, Ireland. Wednesday, 20 August, 2006.

AN ILL WIND BLEW ACROSS the great expanse of The K Club that had nothing to do with the weather. Although high winds had forced Ryder Cup organisers to delay spectator access to the course until mid-morning on the second day of practice, a potentially more serious storm had brewed overnight when Tiger Woods, the world's number one golfer, had been made aware of a supposedly satirical article that appeared in an Irish magazine.

Woods was upset by what he saw in the *Dubliner* magazine, so much so that he brought forward his scheduled media conference by a day. Woods didn't mince his words when he sat behind the microphone. He dropped his signature diplomacy to hit out at the article which appeared under the headline, 'Ryder Cup Filth for Ireland,' and which was accompanied by a photograph of a topless woman that the magazine contended to be Woods' wife, Elin. Such photographs had been circulating on the internet for several years and were dismissed as fakes by Woods' representatives.

What really offended Woods was the magazine's insinuations that his wife could be 'found in a variety of sweaty poses on porn sites across the web.'

As reporters from various media outlets around the world filed into the media conference room for what they thought was a routine conference brought forward because of the weather, Woods took control and opened the press conference by saying, 'I just want to make an opening statement, real quick. That, you know, for me personally, and for my wife, things that have occurred over here, I'm very disappointed. Not the fans, not the people here, not the Irish people. But very disappointed in the article that was written. My wife, yes, she has been a model and she did do some bikini photos. But to link her to porn web sites and such is unacceptable and I do not accept that at all. Neither does our team. And I just want to say that doesn't deter or detract from the beauty of this event.'

He continued: 'The people here have been absolutely fantastic. Irish people have come out and supported us, and Europeans … [but] it's very hard to be diplomatic about this when you have so much emotion involved, and my wife is involved like this.'

Woods had met Elin Nordegren, the daughter of a Swedish government minister, at the British Open at Lytham in 2001 and the couple were married at the Sandy Lane resort in Barbados in 2004. Woods explained why he felt it necessary to come out with all guns blazing in defence of his wife after the article, which the magazine subsequently apologised for publishing claiming it as 'inappropriate', first appeared.

'You do things for the people you love and care about. My wife and I, we're a team and we're in it together. We do things together and I care about her with all my heart.'

With his wife's honour defended, Woods moved on to golfing matters. In past Ryder Cups, he had been willing to allow the likes of Davis Love and Fred Couples assume the role of leaders. He had adopted a different approach in the run-up to this match though, as when he took the four American 'rookies' out to dinner during the WGC-Bridgestone Invitational in Akron and, although sticking to his own practice routines on the range, in tandem with caddie Steve Williams, Woods had taken to the team room with a gusto, dominating the ping-pong table that had been put into the entertainments room.

Although he was the greatest golfer of his generation, Woods' Ryder Cup record—7 wins-11 losses-2 halved matches—before the match at The K Club was poor. In four previous appearances, he had been on the losing team three times. It was an alien concept to a man who cherishes the 'W' word—winning—more than any other.

Woods' Ryder Cup record was a source of disappointment as he headed into the match. He remarked: 'It's disappointing. I haven't won points on the Cups that I've been on, to win points for my team. I've always felt like it's a two-point swing [when losing a match]. Winning a point, losing a point, it feels like it's two points going the wrong way. And, unfortunately, I've got on the wrong end too many times. It's frustrating, because you feel like you've not only let yourself down, but you've let your team-mate down that you're playing with.'

He added: 'As far as me setting the tone [for the match], I would like to get a point for my team. You know, if and when I get put up, that's my responsibility to get points. And if I play in one match or all five, my responsibility is to get points. Hopefully I can do that this year. In years past, I haven't done that. I tried and unfortunately I just haven't done that. Hopefully this year I can get points.'

What was different about the Woods who arrived in Ireland for the 2006 match compared to the one who showed up at Valderrama and The Belfry and Oakland Hills, the scenes of his three previous defeats in the competition, was that he had assumed the role of leader.

'I think Phil [Mickelson], myself and Jim [Furyk] have taken more of a leadership role, because we are veterans of the team,' admitted Woods in the build–up to the 2006 event.

When he made his Ryder Cup debut in 1997, at Valderrama, Woods was content to let others lead. 'I just sat back and listened and learned. That's what you do, if you're a young person on the team ... one day, if you're in that position, you can take up more of a leadership role and do just as good a job.'

Of the demands of the Ryder Cup, compared to how he prepared for majors and individual tournaments, Woods said: 'The atmosphere is different. You're in a team format, [and] some of the guys haven't played much matchplay before. So, there's different changes: the strategy, the mental outlook that you need for matchplay situations. The overall concept of being on a Ryder Cup team is a lot different to when you're playing as an individual in each and every event ... [and] you're adding the fact that you're playing for your country as well.'

That midpoint of the week wasn't a good one generally for the American team. The high winds had restricted spectator entry to the course until health and safety issues were addressed, but the inclement weather had also caused the US team to revise their practice arrangements. Instead of playing their planned foursomes, the Americans conducted what Lehman devised as a 'fun game' with players playing only short iron approaches to the greens and putting out.

The error of their ways became apparent when they ducked under the ropes midway down the first fairway to start hitting iron shots, only to be greeted by the waft of boos coming from spectators who had gathered in the grandstand around the tee box and who were deprived of watching the American players hit off. It was the first public relations gaffe of the week from Lehman, who put his hands up afterwards to accept responsibility.

That night, the US and European teams attended the black tie Ryder Cup Gala Dinner in the CityWest Hotel where guests sipped Moet & Chandon Rose champagne, Marques de Riscal Limousin (2004) white wine and Marques de Riscal Gran Reserva (1999) red wine. The menu featured a starter of 'Tian of Greencastle Crab', a main course of 'Aromatic Rack of Irish Lamb' with wild mushroom confit, Swede Gratin, carrots and red wine jus, and a selection of desserts that included burnt lemon tart, lemon citrus cheesecake and lemon soufflé. Van Morrison provided the musical entertainment.

But the night didn't run entirely as planned. The dinner was delayed by over an hour due to the late arrival of the two teams, who had travelled by bus, and players were surprised to find that their tables—traditionally cordoned off at similar functions at past Ryder Cups—were open and accessible to other diners, which led to a glut of unseemly autograph hunting.

The US team didn't need to be asked twice to leave when the time came, gladly returning to their team room in the West Wing of the hotel where they duly indulged in the buffalo wings and Haribo jelly sweets which had been laid on for them.

THIRTEEN

The Final Countdown

Co. Kildare, Ireland. Thursday, 21 September, 2006.

IRELAND HAD WAITED A LONG, long time to play host to the Ryder Cup. In the end, it had nothing to do with birthright in finally securing the match for the golf-mad country. It didn't matter that Christy O'Connor Senior had played in the thing ten times, or that a procession of Irish players had found themselves in the right place at the right time down the years to sink the winning putt. Quite simply, it had come down to money, and Dr Michael Smurfit's ability to put together a commercial package that also involved rescuing the once-flagging European Open—the financial input over ten years to that tournament from 1995 to 2005 alone exceeding €22 million—and turning it into one of the PGA European Tour's flagship events. All so that the Ryder Cup could be played in his backyard.

The 36th Ryder Cup was the biggest international sporting event ever held in Ireland. A staging team from the European Tour had moved on to the Palmer Course on 8 July, at a time when the European Open was taking place on the Smurfit Course on the south side of the River Liffey, and commenced building work on temporary structures that resulted in 40,000 square metres of tentage for corporate hospitality, the largest ever seen at a golf tournament in Europe.

On the eve of the match, Smurfit, the man who had conceived the vision of one day bringing the Ryder Cup to land that once was farmland, had a seat of honour in the VIP area in front of the stage that hosted the Opening Ceremony. His dress code for the occasion was a turtle neck shirt with The K Club logo. Politicians and businessmen, those who had thrived in the era of the Celtic Tiger, sat in soft seats and soaked it all in. Ireland had waited a long time for this day, and it was most unlikely that anyone present would ever live to see another Ryder Cup staged in the country.

Also in the crowd that day were Irish players who had contributed much to the rich history of the Ryder Cup. Christy O'Connor Senior stood and waved and acknowledged the applause that came his way. Known simply as 'Himself', O'Connor had played his first Ryder Cup match at the exotically named Thunderbird Golf & Country Club in California in November of 1955. It was a different era back then. The teams consisted of players from Great Britain and Ireland competing against the United States, and O'Connor made his debut on a team that lost 8-4 (one session of foursomes, one session of singles). GB&I's last win in the competition had been in 1933.

O'Connor was to play in every Ryder Cup from that debut in 1955 up to the 1973 match at Muirfield. In all that time, he was only once—at Lindrick Golf Club, outside Sheffield, in 1957—on a winning team, and his finest moment had come with a 7 and 6 singles win over Dow Finsterwald in that match.

Other past Ryder Cup players from Ireland were seated beside O'Connor in front of the stage; men who had played not as frequently as 'Himself' but who had nevertheless savoured victory and made significant contributions. O'Connor's nephew, Christy Junior, had made his Ryder Cup debut at Laurel Valley in Pennsylvania in 1975 and had to wait another 14 years, until the Belfry in 1989, to again play in the competition. But Junior had become as vivid a part of the Ryder Cup as any player in its history, when hitting his famous two-iron approach over water from 229 yards to the 18th green in that match, to defeat Fred Couples and win the trophy for Europe.

That two-iron was subsequently sold by O'Connor for charity, so famous a club did it become on the back of the Galwayman's heroics. 'I'd have hit that particular two-iron thousands of times all year,' he recalled from his seat of honour.

'The thing is, I'd already hit a superb two-iron approach at the 17th and, before that, I'd hit it absolutely perfect at the Par 3 12th hole. So I felt very confident on the 18th. On the fairway at 18, both my caddie and I agreed two-iron was about the right club selection and when that happens, you're usually not far wrong. I knew the shot was going to be good the moment it left the clubface.'

O'Connor had badly wanted to be captain of the European team for the match in Ireland. But it was not to be, and instead he took on an ambassadorial role with AIB Bank, one of the event's sponsorship partners. He may not have been in the thick of the team action, yet the Ryder Cup was very much a part of him. He explained the immensity of the event:

'There is no pressure like the Ryder Cup. You're not only playing for yourself, you're also playing for your family, your country and latterly Europe. An awful lot rides on it. There's no money involved, it is totally about pride. And that should be enough to drive any man.'

The O'Connors were not alone in rising to the crowd. Eamonn Darcy, a four-time Ryder Cup player, rose to his feet when introduced by the master of ceremonies, Sharon Ní Bheoláin. Darcy had crucially beaten Ben Crenshaw in his singles match at Muirfield Village in Columbus, Ohio, in 1987. The greens had been cut very tight that year in the belief that it would benefit the Americans, but it transpired that the Europeans were the better putters and Darcy had closed out his match with a difficult downhill six-footer. It was the first time that a visiting Ryder Cup team had won on American soil.

Philip Walton, too, was acclaimed. Walton had held firm under the most intense of pressure in the 1995 Ryder Cup match at Oak Hill in upstate New York. That was Walton's one and only Ryder Cup appearance, but he made his mark in the competition by defeating Jay Haas in the critical singles match that ensured victory for Europe.

Up on the stage, Des Smyth, a vice-captain to Ian Woosnam, looked down at his old tour pals and joined in the applause. Smyth had played in two Ryder Cups, in 1979 and 1981, both of which had resulted in American wins. Smyth had been touted as a possible captain for The K Club but ultimately had to settle for a support role to Woosnam, who was given a one-cup term with Nick Faldo already pencilled in for the 2008 job at Valhalla in Kentucky.

Smyth, who had remained competitive into his 50s and was still competing on the Champions Tour in the United States, had soldiered on tour with Woosie in the early days of their respective careers. When Woosnam had come in for criticism in Munich for failing to inform players before announcing his 'wild card' picks, Smyth had defended him, and said: 'Everyone has a different style of captaincy. Some guys will go and talk to ten players. That's not Ian's style. It was his decision to pick and he chose to do it his way … he kept his cards close to his chest, [players] knew what they had to do to get on the team.'

Woosnam, Smyth and the other vice-captain Peter Baker had settled into the hotel at the resort a couple of days ahead of the arrival of the two teams. Each knew that the Ryder Cup would be one of the busiest weeks they'd ever put in at a golf tournament, even though not one of them would strike a ball in anger. As Smyth, who had picked the brains of a number of contemporaries who had performed similar duties in the past, put it when speaking about his role:

'I was told, "You're going to be running around like a blue-arsed fly!" Needless to say, I'm preparing myself for a busy week.'

It was good that Smyth got to look out at the crowd and witness the likes of the O'Connors, uncle and nephew, and Darcy and Walton among those past Ryder Cup players rise to their feet that day. Up until late-morning, while the two teams had been concluding their final practice rounds, a serious doubt had existed about whether or not the ceremony could go ahead in its desired location. It would have made a mockery of the occasion if the ceremony had moved indoors.

The previous night, winds had reached up to 100 kph in force and a number of trees on the main avenue through The K Club had fallen. All temporary structures on the course had been abandoned for fear that the winds would cause damage and those people evacuated from the course had been temporarily restrained from going to the bus terminals and car parks when the winds caused hoarding in those areas to be blown away.

The fear was that the grand opening ceremony, a Riverdance of golf with a theme taken from the Book of Kells, would have had to be abandoned and a smaller version, without any of the razzmatazz, held inside away from the predicted poor weather. However, the storms stayed away and the opening ceremony went ahead as planned outdoors on the eve of the contest. The ceremony had, at its centrepiece, a giant golf ball, which opened up to reveal Irish traditional musician Donal Lunny, who had composed the Ryder Cup anthem. It was an impressive appetiser to the main and far more serious event that was to follow over the next three days.

The ceremony, where the President of Ireland, Mary McAleese, performed the opening, was a riot of colour and pageantry that had the so-called WAGS—wives and girlfriends of the players, Team Europe dressed in Italian-designed Canali suits and Team USA in Ralph Lauren—dancing in the aisles.

There were choirs and war-painted dancers, an orchestra and giant carnival figures. It was spectacular and it was fun and it all smacked of an innocence in the midst of overt commerciality. Thousands of spectators massed in front of the stage, little more than an iron shot away from the three-tier corporate hospitality unit that ran down the 18th hole, and the massive merchandise shop that struggled to keep sufficient amounts of apparel; umbrellas, Waterford Crystal and golf balls, all of which bore the Ryder Cup logo, in stock. The masses who had flocked to the course over the practice days bought all before them.

The third and final practice day had set the scene for the real deal, the three days of competition that followed. The crowds were huge, bringing with them an atmosphere previously unknown at practice days in the history of the Ryder Cup. The two teams, as they had done since appearing in public for the first time the previous Tuesday, signed autographs and smiled for the cameras in between playing golf shots. Team USA had blundered the previous day when playing a virtual 12-ball of short shots and putts, rather than partaking in traditional practice, but were back on the charm offensive for the final day of practice.

Earlier that morning, the two teams had assembled to have their official team photographs taken. When David Howell turned up on the 10th green, it emerged that he was wearing the wrong coloured shirt and his blushes were spared by Padraig Harrington's caddie, Ronan Flood, who swapped with him. But when it had come time for the Americans to get their official team photograph taken, a different sort of omission occurred: the Ryder Cup had been taken away by the Europeans, and the US team had to pose without the gold trophy.

The opening ceremony was not just about pomp. There was a more serious side too. The two captains, Tom Lehman and Ian Woosnam, introduced their teams, one by one, and six anthems— those of the United States, Europe, Ireland, Great Britain, Sweden and Spain—were played before the pairings for the first session of play on the Friday were announced.

That Woods and Furyk would play at number one for the Americans was well flagged. Woosnam had suspected that Lehman would send out the two heavy hitters at the start of the order.

'It's going to be a big boost for us if we can beat that pairing,' said Europe's captain in putting up Harrington and Montgomerie, who had taken out Woods and Phil Mickelson in the corresponding match at Oakland Hills.

'I expected Monty to be in that first group with Padraig,' said Lehman after the announcement. 'The first point is a big point, [but] it's not like the first match, whoever wins that match, that the tournament is over. That's not it at all.'

Lehman knew how important it was for his team for Woods to lead from the front. 'The guy is the best player in the world. He proves it over and over again. If he played five matches here like he plays 95 per cent of the major championships, he's going to win four or five points. Judging by how we've done here [in the Ryder Cup] recently, that would be a nice boost.'

The omens had been good that Woods had felt more of a team player going into the contest. As Verplank had put it, 'Tiger's a little less reserved and he's asserting himself a little more socially than he has done in the past. He's kind of buying into this [idea] of having 11 buddies with him for a week instead of, you know, me against the world. He's actually a very good guy ... I could see how it is hard for him to let down some of his guard and fall under somebody else's schedule or plan, but I think he understands that to play well in this event, that's what he has got to do. I think he's making some steps to do that.'

Woods was just one man, but a vital part of the American machine. Cink was more aware than most of his importance to the team. 'As far as Tiger's record not being great [in the Ryder Cup], I think the [European] team rises up to play against him.

They see him, you cut off the head of the dragon … he's the head, our number one player, no question. But Tiger is tired of losing, like we all are. That's one thing about Tiger. He does not like to lose at anything, whether it is golf or ping-pong or billiards or a spitting contest. Whatever it is, he does not want to lose and he is tired of it. He's going to put his best foot forward here.'

But Woods was just one player on a team of 12 and, Woosnam, who had grown into the role of captain as the week had progressed, showed a tough streak of his own straight away, omitting Luke Donald, David Howell and Henrik Stenson from his fourballs. McGinley, who had struggled with his form over the summer, was the other omission.

'Very difficult,' said Woosnam of his task to inform players that they wouldn't be playing. 'I've got nine players in the top 25 in the world and it is difficult to tell players they are not playing. That's the trouble we've got.'

But Woosnam had also come up with a potential dream team. In the late 1980s and 1990s, José María Olazábal had teamed-up with Seve Ballesteros in a partnership that became known as the Spanish Armada. Woosie saw a new version, putting Sergio García together with Olazábal. The two Spaniards had never previously partnered each other, a fact mainly due to Olazábal appearing in the event for the first time since 1999.

'Olazábal has been around for a long time. He has a lot of experience, and the enthusiasm that he has shown all week has been incredible. Keeping him off the golf course has been the hardest problem … and Sergio's been around a while now and he's such a fantastic player. They are just going to work beautifully together,' explained Woosnam of his reasoning in putting the two men together. David Toms and 'rookie' Brett Wetterich would provide their opposition.

Lehman had decided to blood two of his rookies. JJ Henry, who had been feted in front of 45,000 spectators at a college football match at his alma mater at Texas Christian University the week before he landed in Ireland, was paired with Stewart Cink for the second fourballs match against Paul Casey and Robert Karlsson.

But the largest roar of all at the opening ceremony greeted the announcement that Darren Clarke would play in the first session of fourballs. All week, Clarke had played alongside his fellow 'wild card' pick Lee Westwood in practice, and Woosie caused no real surprise when announcing that they would play in the bottom match against Mickelson and DiMarco. 'It's going to be a difficult match, not just because Lee and Darren are such incredibly talented players, but because of the emotions involved,' attested Mickelson.

The practice ground had been transformed into the venue for the opening ceremony, and it was here that the two captains addressed the crowd that featured what was a cross-section of European society. Lehman had a tear in his eye as he looked at the flag-raising ceremony.

'There is such a strong bond, a strong connection between the United States and between Ireland; so much of our country's history has been shaped by men and women with origins in this country, and I think it is only fitting that we celebrate this Ryder Cup right here this year and I am so honoured to be here … we promise to give you an event that you'll always remember, filled with sportsmanship, with compassion, with fierce competition, but with more than anything, mutual respect,' he told the crowd.

Woosnam's greatest fear when he assumed the role of Europe's captain, had been public speaking. He was a man of actions, not words. And, following on from Lehman, an accomplished and eloquent speaker, he took a deep breath. His words were honest, and from the heart. Woosnam, a Celt, opened with the traditional Irish greeting, of 'Céad Mile Fáilte, one hundred thousand welcomes.' He was immediately relaxed.

'You have waited a very long time for the Ryder Cup to come to Ireland and, as we all know, Ireland is famous for its hospitality and famous for its craic and for giving us so many great names that have played in the Ryder Cup … this week's venue, The K Club, is an absolutely spectacular setting for such an historic match … and continue the traditions which has passed from one generation to another since Samuel Ryder presented this magnificent trophy for competition. In 1927, Walter Hagen and Ted Ray stood as Ryder Cup captains for the very first time and, now, 79 years later, Tom and I are very proud and honoured to follow them and write another chapter in the history of his great event,' said Woosnam.

'This week is all about honour and tradition, sportsmanship and integrity, and we stand here knowing that we are playing with pride and passion for the honour of holding the Cup. May the best team win.'

The Americans had forgotten how to win in the Ryder Cup, the gap having gotten larger and larger with each passing year. While the European team had watched their inspirational video, Lehman felt it would be a good idea if each of his players sang their college 'fight song'. Lehman himself sang the Minnesota Gophers song. What had seemed like a good idea, however, backfired when it transpired many of the players didn't actually know all of the words to their college songs. It was all a bit of fun before the serious stuff got under way. They also hoped that the inadequacies of their singing wouldn't transfer itself to the golf course.

FOURTEEN

Flying Start

Co. Kildare, Ireland. Friday, 22 September, 2006.

THE CONCEPT OF A PARK and ride system was alien to those Irish people who attended sporting events, but the success of the procedure that had taken years of planning was evident on the first official morning of the Ryder Cup. Spectators, many of whom had won the prized tickets on an internet lottery conducted by the European Tour, moved in the dark of morning from shuttle buses parked in the North Terminal, and, having had their tickets and photo identification checked by the heavy security presence, filed through the entrance gates.

The u-shaped grandstand that hugged the first tee had filled soon after the gates had opened at 7am, and crowds, five and six deep in places, lined the first fairway all the way down to the green, 418 yards from the tee. It was an incredible scene.

The storm, the remnants of Hurricane Gordon, had hit the previous night but dispersed in time for the long-anticipated match, although those who made the early pilgrimage to the course were reminded that it would be wise to have wet-gear close to hand, as the sun struggled to break through the blanket of grey cloud overhead.

There had been a huge amount of rainfall over the preceding few days, with the consequence that a policy of 'lift, clean and place' was adopted on the fairways. A decision on implementing such conditions had been deferred until the first day of actual play. All week in practice, balls had been picking up mud, in spite of the pristine nature of the fairways, which had been tended into excellent condition by the greens superintendent Gerry Byrne.

At the previous week's Lumber Classic on the PGA Tour, mud balls had been an unwelcome feature after a decision had been taken not to implement preferred lies. The result was that balls squirted off at peculiar angles, and neither Tom Lehman nor Ian Woosnam wished to see a recurrence of that in the Ryder Cup. As Lehman put it at the time: 'Do you want to see a bunch of mud balls squirting and going dead sideways? I don't think everybody wants to see that. It would be more fun to watch the guys have their chance to hit good shots.'

· · · ·

AFTER YEARS OF WAITING FOR the moment, the time had come. The hands on the Rolex clock by the first tee had just passed 7.50am when the hooting and hollering noises from the practice range, a short 150 yards walk across the avenue from the first tee, grew louder and louder. It could mean only one thing: the players were on the way.

When Tiger Woods and Jim Furyk, wearing grey patterned slip-on tops, made it on to the first tee, their captain was waiting for them. The handshakes were a courtesy. Each of their faces were strained, an indication that the practice was over and that the real thing had arrived.

What had been a noisy cauldron for the top American pairing turned louder a couple of minutes later as Colin Montgomerie and Padraig Harrington, appropriately dressed in green, strode onto the tee.

Monty, who thought he had done and seen it all at Ryder Cups, shook his head in wonderment. The man lampooned as 'Mrs

Doubtfire' on his many travels to majors in the United States, the man American fans loved to hate, was serenaded by an adoring home crowd and, when Ivor Robson, the starter, finally brought a moment's quiet to quell the chorus of 'Ole-Ole-Ole,' it had been to introduce Woods. A respectful quiet greeted Robson's announcement that the world's number one was on the tee, about to start the match.

The first shot of the 36th Ryder Cup also provided the first twist. Woods pull-hooked a tee shot like a mere mortal and watched in disbelief as the ball curled farther and farther left until it splashed into the lake. The Ryder Cup had begun, but not the way people had expected. European players on the driving range had halted their pre-round routines to watch Woods' opening drive on the Jumbotron television screen and some allowed themselves wry grins as the ball hooked its way to a watery grave. It was evidence, if it were needed, that nobody was immune from the pressure of the Ryder Cup.

One by one that morning, Robson had introduced the players. Match by match, players teed off. Each player, each match, had been greeted by roars normally found in football stadiums, not at golf courses. The final match of the morning fourballs featured Darren Clarke and Lee Westwood against Phil Mickelson and Chris DiMarco. If anything, the noise decibel level increased to a height that hadn't previously been heard all that morning. The reason was Clarke.

Clarke and Westwood knew what would await them on the first tee and had delayed their arrival until the last moment possible, but they still reached the tee ahead of their American opponents. They were the first European fourball to do so. Westwood reached the tee marginally ahead of Clarke. The reception they received caused the hairs to stand on their necks. 'I was nearly crying and looked at Billy [Foster], and he was nearly crying. That made me worse,' recalled Westwood.

The reception had been greater than even Clarke had anticipated. Each of the other players, in turn, gave him a hug.

'If I can have two guys like Phil Mickelson and Chris DiMarco giving me hugs on the first tee, that is what the Ryder Cup is all about. It's not about animosity, it's about a match we both want to win amongst friends,' said Clarke later that day.

When his turn had come to tee off, Clarke wasn't found wanting. He hit a booming drive down the middle of the fairway, just short of the hazard, and fired a wedge approach to ten feet. He holed the birdie putt, and Europe had gone one up.

. . . .

JIM FURYK, WHO HAD SINGLE-handedly taken the weight of the moment on to his shoulders, saved Tiger Woods' embarrassment on the first hole in the top fourball match. His swing—instilled in him from a young age by his dad, Mike, the only coach that he'd ever worked with—had been the cause of much mirth throughout his career. The late Jim Murray once observed that he'd seen 'more form on a guy fighting a swarm of bees'.

But it was a swing that had served Furyk well, winning him a US Open in 2003 and getting him as high as number two in the world rankings after his win in the Canadian Open just two weeks prior to the Ryder Cup.

Furyk had been the first player from either team to arrive at The K Club, something that had been brought about by his early exit in the previous week's World Matchplay in London, and the extra time seemed to have been well spent when he responded to Woods' wild first drive by birdying the first hole—against pars from Padraig Harrington and Colin Montgomerie—to put the USA one up.

Furyk was to be the rock that Woods leaned on for much of the morning. On the fifth, Woods provided another hint at human frailty when he missed a short par putt that enabled the Europeans to draw level. When Woods grabbed his first birdie of the round, on the Par 3 eighth hole, Furyk seemed so relieved that his man was back in the game that he hugged him. Woods barely acknowledged his friend's gesture, and kept his own game face on.

By the time the four players walked off the 12th hole, Woods had broken the back of the match with two successive long birdie putts that left the Americans three up. And, although Harrington and Montgomerie rallied, coming home with birdies on the 14th and 16th, Woods and Furyk claimed the top match by a 2 Holes margin. Woods and Furyk shook hands firmly and clapped each other on the back, their job done. The ubiquitous Lehman materialised long enough to offer his congratulations to his new 'dream team,' players who had carried on their form from the previous year's President's Cup match. Michael Jordan, the basketball legend and a friend of Woods, also passed on his congratulations.

That was as good as it got for the visiting team in the first session of fourball matches. Woosnam had greeted each one of his team as they walked onto the first tee and, a la Seve Ballesteros at Valderrama in 1997, had then taken to the captain's buggy so that he could be in the thick of the action. Unlike Ballesteros, who went as far as to tell players what shot they should hit and how they should execute it, Woosnam's approach was not so in their faces. He let them know he was there, but only rarely ventured to impart any information apart from offering encouragement.

Only once all morning did Woosie attempt to provide any advice to any of his players. It happened in the second fourball match, where Robert Karlsson and Paul Casey were one-up playing the Par 4 seventh hole, known as 'Michael's Favourite' but a hole which had caused all manner of club selection problems for the first match that went through. The wind blew straight down the fairway, into the faces of the players, and the lake in front of the green had already garnered a couple of extra new golf balls when the second group of players faced up to their shots.

As he was entitled to do, Woosnam told Karlsson that the players ahead had underestimated the strength of the wind. The captain recommended to the Swede that he take an extra club, which was precisely what Karlsson did. The result was far from perfect. Karlsson's approach was beautifully struck and cleared the water that guarded the green, but it also airmailed the putting surface and bounced up to the top of the television gantry behind the green. A startled Sky Sports cameraman didn't know what to do, deciding it was best to let the ball lie where it had come to rest at his feet.

Karlsson was highly fortunate not to be out of bounds. Once the ball had been retrieved from the feet of the cameraman, identified and thrown back down to terra firma, he was given a free drop. Lehman, who had appeared on the scene, was not best pleased that Karlsson was afforded the drop in front of the gantry rather than to the side. However, it was deemed that the drop area was not closer to the flag and the match referee allowed Karlsson to make it. He still faced a very difficult pitch, out of rough and with not much green to work with to get the ball close to the flag. But, riding his luck, he proceeded to get up and down for a winning par that put Europe two-up.

However, Woosnam had learned his lesson and, instead of offering any more advice on club selection, he let the players and caddies work things out for themselves. Instead, Woosie got back to doing what he did best; offering encouraging, using his electric buggy to whizz from one match to another.

Karlsson and Casey proceeded to go three-up at the turn, only for JJ Henry and Cink to produce a tremendous fightback on the homeward journey. The Americans claimed five birdies in six holes from the 10th hole to go one-up on the European duo by the time they walked off the 15th green. Casey finally stopped the rot by holing a long birdie putt on the 16th. It levelled matters, which was how it finished: a halved match.

• • • •

WHEN THE US TEAM HAD paid a post-Akron two-day bonding trip to the Straffan, the rumour mill had murmured that Wetterich had somehow found a course that fitted his eye. The word was that he had discovered angles on holes that other players simply hadn't seen, because of his length off the tee. The word was that he could become the secret weapon in America's arsenal. Unfortunately for Wetterich, his first tee shot in his debut match had all the accuracy of a misdirected missile, when he pushed the drive into trees. It became an all too familiar plight for Wetterich, a native of Cincinnati, who quickly discovered that practice and the competition are two different things.

All morning, Wetterich and his fourballs partner David Toms had searched in vain for the impetus that would sink the Spanish duo of García and Olazábal. Eventually, the match finished on the 16th green—a 3 and 2 win in favour of the Europeans—with 'El Nino', aka 'The Kid,' having assumed the role of inspirational leader.

García had been quite superb, his ball-striking immaculate. The first fairway he missed in what turned out to be an exhibition of driving had been on the 10th, at which stage he and Olazábal had moved into a two-hole lead. They literally cruised to victory, García rubbing salt into the American wounds with a birdie-birdie close out. 'We gelled beautifully,' he enthused.

Prior to the match, Woosnam had compared García to a Spanish bull. He obviously took it to heart, putting a head cover in the guise of a bull onto his driver. García lay down a marker from the start when he smacked a 297 yards drive off the first tee, just short of the drain that worked its way across the fairway and in front of the green. He followed with an approach that left the ball on the edge of the green and he rolled in the birdie putt, which gave them a lead that was never to be relinquished in a match where the two Spaniards dominated.

Even the great and the mighty savoured García's magical play that opening morning, as he responded like only he could to the adulation of the crowds. Spanish, Irish and European flags unfurled all the way round the course, on tees and at greenside, to hail the magnetic duo. And, on the seventh hole, a treacherous Par 4 that provided a watery grave for many players in the fourball matches, García, who could do no wrong, hit a beautiful iron approach on to the green. Dr Smurfit, who stood behind the Spaniard on the fairway as the player sent his shot on the way to the green, gained the best view in the house.

It proved to be a miserable debut for Wetterich. An incident on the 11th green highlighted his lot. When Toms managed to hole a 30-foot birdie putt there, Wetterich went to high-five his team-mate—and missed! When García answered Toms' birdie with one of his own, the perfectly synchronised high-five that García and Olazábal exchanged was a thing of beauty, and simply affirmed how in unison the two players were in their quest for fourballs victory.

On the signature 16th hole, with the approach over the river, García's three-iron second shot found the green. The noise from those gathered in the giant grandstand by the Liffey could have been heard in his native Castellón.

'It made me shiver, I had goose bumps down the back of my neck,' he was to remark afterwards.

It had been an emotional return to Ryder Cup action for Olazábal after a seven years absence. In the past, Olazábal was the younger partner of the original Spanish Armada with Seve Ballesteros.

'So, how did a return to Ryder Cup fare compare?' he was asked.

'It's different. When you're 21 years old and you are playing your first Ryder Cup. You have your whole future ahead of you. You're just happy to be there, and really nervous. I was shaking like a leaf on the first tee at Muirfield [in 1978], playing alongside Seve. But the way you see it is different. Now, you know there's not many more Ryder Cups in you, and you try to enjoy every minute of it. You know you are very privileged to be part of it.'

On the 16th, with the match point sown up, Olazábal put his arms around García. 'Today was a very special one,' he said to his young compatriot, 'and the way you played was awesome.'

On another day, Olazábal's return to Ryder Cup duty after a long, seven-year gap would have provided the heartstring story. On that Friday morning, however, Darren Clarke's return had no rival. Playing as a captain's pick just six weeks after his wife's death, Clarke attempt to find solace in his golf. He had struck first blood with a birdie at the first hole to go one-up with Westwood over Mickelson and DiMarco in the final fourball match of the first session of play.

Maybe the Americans sensed that things would not go their way when, on the third hole, after initially leaving his first attempt in the bunker, Westwood holed out with his second sand shot for a par to halve the hole. But, by the turn, the match was all-square again and each side matched par with par and birdie with birdie until the decisive moment of the match was provided by Clarke at the 16th hole.

The 16th, a Par 5 of 555 yards, was a risk and reward hole in the finest Arnold Palmer tradition. The onus was, firstly, placed on the player to find the fairway. If he did so, there was an opportunity to reach the island green set in the River Liffey in two shots. If he missed the fairway off the tee, the only option was for a player to lay up and to take his chances of getting up and down for birdie. Clarke had hit a magnificent drive, and was left with 252 yards to the flag. Destiny was calling him.

He deliberated for a time with his caddie, Billy Foster, who had served in good times and bad with his boss. Nobody knew Clarke's on-course mood better than his faithful bagman. The debate was not whether or not he would go for the green—that was always his intention—but on what club the player should use for the task. Clarke finally settled on his five-wood, a fairway metal that had served him well through the years.

There was no greater stage than the 16th to hit the shot that Clarke conjured up that morning. The huge grandstands were packed, with not a spare seat to be found, and Clarke's approach found the green, never once looking as if it would go off course and finish in the water as others had done so often during European Opens. The shot was faultless, and he followed by sinking the birdie putt. It put Clarke and Westwood one-up, with two holes to play, but their work had not yet been completed.

DiMarco, for his part, showed his fighting qualities with a par on the 17th after Mickelson had put his drive into the water. It was enough to send the match down to the final hole, where it took another tremendous five-wood shot from Clarke on the 18th hole, another Par 5, before the win was secured. Clarke again found the fairway off his drive and, faced with an approach of 242 yards to the flag set in the back right corner, the Dungannon man hit his second shot to the apron of the green, no more than 12 feet from the hole. He almost sank the eagle putt, but the conceded birdie was sufficient to make his first match in the 2006 Ryder Cup a winning one.

'The reception I received on the first tee will live with me forever,' Clarke recalled after his morning win. 'I don't know if it begins the healing, or helps, or whatever … but I'm very proud to be a part of this team and to be here. Time is the only thing that can help me heal and I am doing the best that I can.'

·   ·   ·   ·

WOOSNAM, LIKE LEHMAN, HAD BEEN required to produce his foursome pairings for the second session of matches at midday, some time before the fourball matches had concluded. When Europe's captain handed in his team-sheet, it included the four men who had been idle in the morning fourball matches. It meant that, for the first time since Tony Jacklin in the 1983 match at Palm Beach Gardens in Florida, a European captain had utilised all 12 of his players on the first day. It was a brave move from Woosie, but also showed the level of confidence that he had in his team. He had sent out a signal that there were no weak links.

The four European players who had undertaken cheerleading duty in the morning were Luke Donald, Henrik Stenson, David Howell and Paul McGinley. That Woosnam had been able to leave three players ranked in the world's top 15 in reserve provided an indication of the strength in depth that he had in his team. More than that, there had not been a single murmur of dissent from any of those benched in the fourballs.

All had appeared on the first tee that morning to see off their team-mates and had followed different matches for a considerable time before moving on to the range to prepare for their own afternoon matches.

Lehman didn't have the same luxury as Woosnam. The American side was top-heavy. It had the top three players in the world rankings but, as previous Ryder Cups had shown, that statistic alone was no guarantee of success. When Lehman revealed his hand for the foursomes, two players—Scott Verplank and Vaughn Taylor—were again left out of the loop.

The body language in the European camp was different. Clarke, who had won the final fourball with Westwood to ensure that Europe won the first session by 2 ½ points to 1 ½ points, had put his hand up when Woosnam looked for a volunteer to sit out the foursomes. The gesture had been another sign of the harmony that existed in the European camp. The fall-out that Thomas Bjørn had predicted had failed to materialise.

The crowds, who had gathered around the 18th green as Clarke and Westwood finished off Mickelson and DiMarco in the fourballs, stayed just long enough to soak up the scene. But not too long. The foursomes matches had already started before Clarke's birdie putt was conceded, and many of those who had watched that act moved swiftly on to the next phase of the engagement.

Padraig Harrington, who had barely ten minutes from the time that he finished his fourball match to the time that he started his foursomes, had been paired-up with his old sparring partner Paul McGinley for the first match of the afternoon, against Chad Campbell and Zach Johnson. That fourball had been a slow affair and had taken almost five and a half hours to complete. Harrington didn't have much time to access the menu between matches. He loaded up with a bowl of fruit and shepherds pie, and headed out again.

The foursomes, where players played alternate shots, was a much quicker format than the fourballs, and those spectators who moved from the conclusion of the Clarke-Westwood match on the 18th to the first hole joined the match just as the two Americans birdied to take the lead.

Woosnam had intentionally sent out Harrington and McGinley at the front of the proceedings, hoping that they would feed off the energy of the huge Irish support. The two were experienced Ryder Cup players, having featured on the previous two winning teams, and McGinley—who had been a very good Gaelic footballer in his youth and revelled in team environments—had become one of the most articulate and honest guys to have in any team room. This Ryder Cup meant a lot to him. He had battled injury and poor form in the months running up to the event but a measure of his determination to do well was the fact that McGinley, whether with coach Bob Torrance or short game guru Pete Cowan, had been the last player on the range most nights in the run-up to the contest.

McGinley badly wanted this Ryder Cup to be memorable in an already impressive career CV. He wanted to use the crowd that afternoon.

'There's two ways of going with adrenalin; you can go with the motion and ride it or you can try to keep yourself very calm. It's one of two ways. Neither way is right, neither way is wrong,' he remarked. 'I think we fed off the crowd, as passionate as they were.'

Although the Americans took the early lead in the match, it didn't last long. On the short third hole, Harrington rolled in a birdie putt after McGinley's tee shot finished 15 feet from the hole. On the fourth hole, a downhill Par 5 of 568 yards, it was McGinley's turn to roll in a winning birdie to put the two home players from Rathfarnham in south Dublin into the lead. Their lead, however, was short-lived.

McGinley and Harrington turned all-square with Campbell and Johnson. The Europeans went one-up on the 11th, and two-up on the 15th. Two holes up with three to play, destiny was in their own hands. The crowds grew louder, more expectant. The finishing three holes on the course included two Par 5s, which made it a swing stretch in matchplay, and it was here that the stubborn visitors provided the sucker punches.

Nobody played the final holes as well as Campbell and Johnson, who finished birdie-birdie-birdie to the par-birdie-par finish of the two Irishmen. The match was halved.

'It's top-class golf,' observed McGinley of the American comeback, 'and that's what happens [in the Ryder Cup]. You've got to give credit to the American boys, finishing with three birdies. We played well. Our figures were good and we would have won a lot of the games out there.'

Harrington was physically drained when he finished. He had been first onto the tee that morning, along with Colin Montgomerie, at 8am, and it was 6.10pm when his foursomes match finished, for the second time that day, on the 18th green. He had played 36 holes of matchplay under the most intense pressure that any player could face. He had been over ten hours on the course, ten hours of being cheered and encouraged and all the time focusing on the task. His meagre reward had been a half point from a possible two.

'My legs are tired, yeah, very tired. It's very heavy on the legs and it is the Ryder Cup, so you're pacing around all day,' said Harrington. But he wouldn't have missed it for the world.

· · · ·

HENRIK STENSON HAD WAITED A long time to make his Ryder Cup debut. The Swede had all but booked his place on Woosnam's team when winning the Qatar Masters as early as the previous January. He was enjoying a rich vein of form, so much so that Paul Broadhurst, who had failed in his own quest to make the European team, was to remark of Stenson, 'He's the next special one from Europe.'

Stenson's form had dipped over the summer but, with an almost perfect sense of timing, he had won the BMW International in Munich and then took two weeks off to get ready for his rookie appearance for Europe. That morning, Stenson, like David Howell, had been present on the first tee as the first wayward ball of the match had been struck by Tiger Woods.

But theirs had been a watching and supporting brief, not a playing one. It had, however, given them a chance to savour the atmosphere of the occasion and Stenson and Howell were paired together for the second foursomes match that afternoon, where they faced David Toms and Stewart Cink.

Toms and Cink had both played in the first session of fourball matches, but neither had won. Toms was on the wrong end of a drubbing from the Spanish Armada, while Cink at least had salvaged a game halved point in his match with JJ Henry against Robert Karlsson and Paul Casey. The Cink-Toms partnership had been one that Lehman had in mind from the time he gave one of his picks to Cink on the morning after the PGA Championship in Medinah in August, but the Casey-Stenson partnership was one that had only come about for Woosnam after watching the two players in practice in the days running up to the match.

By playing Stenson in the foursomes, Woosnam had also managed to give all 12 of his players an outing on the first day of competition. He had 'blooded' all of his men. What transpired in the second foursomes was a high quality match where, quite unbelievably in this alternate shot format, only one bogey was recorded. It was impressive golf. Cink and Toms had grabbed the initiative on the second hole with a birdie to move one-up, but the lead lasted only as long as it took for the players to play the short third hole.

On the Par 3 third hole, Howell, who had been troubled by a shoulder injury in the weeks preceding the contest, hit a fine tee shot that left his partner with a five-foot birdie putt. Stenson sank the putt to immediately square the match. The momentum was with the European pair, and, on the fourth, it was Howell's turn to sink the birdie putt that put Europe one-up for the first time in the match.

Again, in what would be a tight match all the way through, the lead short-lived. Toms, recognised as one of the top putters on the PGA Tour, rolled in a winning birdie putt on the fifth and the teams were to remain on level-pegging in par golf all the way to the 10th hole, a Par 5, where Stenson's length off the tee was a crucial factor. Howell converted his five-footer for birdie there, which regained a one-hole advantage for the Europeans.

After that, it was back to impressive foursomes par golf from both teams for the next four holes, until the 15th. The Par 4 of 446 yards had a lake running down the right, in play for any pushed drive. As soon as Howell hit his tee-shot, he knew it was destined for trouble and the groans from the huge galleries confirmed that the ball would not be seen again, unless it was to reappear as a novelty souvenir. Stenson and Howell failed to save par and, with Cink and Toms on the green in two, the Americans were conceded their birdie putt to go back all-square again.

Both teams had chances to win the match over the closing stretch of holes. On the 16th, Toms' approach cleared the river and finished in a greenside trap, from where Cink played a majestic bunker shot that resulted in a conceded birdie. The bunker shot put significant pressure on the Europeans, who had somehow missed landing in the same trap on their approach and, instead, had finished up in thick greenside rough. But Stenson, more noted for his power game, also showed a deft touch with a beautifully played chip to two feet which Howell holed for a halved hole.

Each shot, each putt, from both teams, was greeted with appreciation from the galleries. On the 17th, Toms, had a chance to win the hole, but his birdie putt refused to drop. It all came down to the 18th. Again, Toms had a birdie chance, from 22 feet, only for the ball to hang on the lip. It was promptly conceded. And, then, Howell's 20-footer for birdie did the exact same thing. That, too, was immediately conceded. Stenson's Ryder Cup debut had not produced a win, but it produced a halved match.

· · · ·

A SIMPLE MATTER OF LOGISTICS had determined that the foursomes match between Sergio García and Luke Donald, and Tiger Woods and Jim Furyk, jump ahead of the scheduled third foursomes in the order of play. The morning fourballs had been very slow, to the point that Lee Westwood, Phil Mickelson and Chris DiMarco were still on-course playing at a time when Ivor Robson should have been announcing their names on the first tee for the afternoon foursomes.

In truth, it didn't really matter what order the match was played in. Effectively, it pitted Europe's top-two players in the world rankings against the top, most in-form players on the American team. For Donald, who had not played in the morning, it represented a baptism of fire at this Ryder Cup. García had been in scintillating form in partnering Olazábal to victory in the fourball, and Woods—although struggling a bit on the greens— had eventually got the job done with Furyk in his fourball match.

Donald's last time to play with Woods had been in the final round of the PGA Championship and he had failed miserably that day to come up to the task. The Englishman's first tee-shot of the Ryder Cup didn't inspire too much confidence; a wayward effort that finished up in the trees.

'I think when you miss the morning and come straight into the foursomes, there's a lot more pressure on individual shots,' Donald was to observe.

But Donald wasn't the only one who had found trouble on that first hole. For much of the morning, Furyk had been the strong hand in his fourball with Woods. On this first hole of foursomes, though, Furyk, one of the most reliable players in the game, had pushed his drive into the trees. What's more, it couldn't have found a worse lie, finishing barely a couple of inches away from a tree trunk and offered Woods no prospect of getting a proper shot at the ball.

Woods had to become something of a magician in attempting to play the recovery shot, taking a wedge and twisting the club around so that he played the shot left-handed. It was a shot beyond even the capabilities of the world's top player. Woods moved the ball no more than four feet. With the ball still immersed in thick rough,

Furyk's next shot—the pair's third—found greenside rough, from where Woods played out to 15 feet. When Furyk missed the bogey putt, Europe, eight feet from the hole in three, were conceded the hole.

That opening blip from Furyk was corrected by the third hole, won in par, which restored parity. But it didn't last long. García, long and accurate as he had been in the fourballs that morning, set up a winning birdie on the Par 5 fourth. It gave Europe the lead again, and one that was never taken from them.

Still one-up at the turn, Donald and García also won the 10th where Woods missed a five-footer for par. García and Donald looked at each other, and allowed each other a discreet grin. As they walked to the 11th tee, the galleries raised the tempo even higher, if that was possible. It was to be a case of nip'n'tuck for the next few holes, the US reducing the deficit on the 11th where García's wedge approach from 139 yards was so poor that he left the unfortunate Donald with no shot from the rough. The Englishman failed to find the green with his recovery, and their advantage fell to just one hole.

All the while, García and Donald waited for the fightback from men who detested losing. They were not required to wait much longer. When Woods rolled in a birdie putt to win the 13th, and then Furyk rolled in a three-footer for birdie to claim the 14th to go all-square, it seemed as if the USA had all of the momentum, as they headed into the closing stretch of holes that would make or break the tie. After the 15th hole was halved, García's magical touch returned on the 16th when he hit a sand wedge approach of 108 yards to within 18 inches. Furyk bravely sank an eight-footer to halve the hole.

On the 17th, a hole known as 'Half Moon' for the way that it curled around the banks of the River Liffey, García's nine-iron approach to five-feet set Donald up for birdie and, after Furyk's 12-footer for birdie slipped by the hole, the Englishman kept his composure to hole the putt. The passion exuded by García spread to Donald, who allowed himself a clenched fist to the masses packed around the green.

The 18th hole on the Palmer Course, a risk-and-reward Par 5, was a classic matchplay finishing hole and, although the Europeans had an edge, Woods' superb drive left Furyk with 228 yards to the pin and an opportunity to put pressure on the Anglo-Spanish duo. But, just as he had done on the first hole, Furyk did the unexpected.

There were no trees to cause havoc. Instead, it was a pulled long-iron by Furyk into the water on the hole known as the 'Hooker's Graveyard' that proved destructive. On they trudged and, after taking a penalty drop, Woods' fourth shot finished 18 feet from the hole. García's third shot, a chip, finished off the back of the green, but Donald's par putt finished close to the hole and, with no way back, the match was conceded by the Americans.

'I made a bad swing, caught the ball on the toe and got it hooking. I just did everything you shouldn't do,' said Furyk, while Woods conceded: 'We just weren't able to get it together.'

'I'm just really lucky, I get really good team-mates,' replied García when quizzed afterwards about his Ryder Cup record, that, after the first afternoon's endeavours had resulted in a career improvement to seven foursomes wins from seven since he made his team debut in 1999.

The broadest smile, as players high-fived, and Woosnam congratulated the two men beside the 18th green, belonged to García.

'I just love the Ryder Cup. I couldn't live without it. It's just amazing. I guess that drives me even harder in this event,' he enthused.

Woosnam couldn't have asked for more from García. 'You know, he just lifted his game unbelievably, which he always seems to do when he plays in the Ryder Cup. He has that spirit, that Spanish spirit … he's on top form.'

García was giddy and delighted afterwards, until stopped in his tracks by an inquisitor in the post-foursomes press conference. The questions came thick and fast to García, but one, in Spanish, prompted an answer, in Spanish, that left everyone but his questioner confused and seemed to have no end. Eventually, Luke Donald, his foursomes partner, nudged García, the player who had become the life and soul of the European team.

'I can't stop. He's just been telling me that I've been playing shit and I'm trying to make him realise I'm having a pretty decent summer,' remarked García to his colleague-in-arms. How anyone, on that day of days, could have questioned García's form beggared belief. In both fourball and foursomes, García had been inspirational.

· · · ·

THE FINAL FOURSOMES MATCH OF the first afternoon's play involved Colin Montgomerie and Lee Westwood—two Ryder Cup veterans paired together for a first time as Woosnam again demonstrated a willingness to try new things—against Phil Mickelson and Chris DiMarco, a partnership that had evolved in the 2005 President's Cup but which had only the sour taste of defeat from the morning foursomes to take into a rushed lunch before reappearing on the first tee.

There was no obvious order to the early part of the contest, as holes were swapped with all the giddiness of children trading cards in a schoolyard. The Americans were one up after the first, the Europeans one hole ahead by the time they left the fourth and the Americans back in front by the time the four players walked off the sixth green, where Mickelson and DiMarco had dampened the spirits of the huge European support with a winning par.

On the seventh, Monty brought some semblance of order to affairs, with an outrageous par putt. Westwood had left his partner some 30 feet from the hole but Montgomerie rammed the ball home and didn't even consider approaching the hole to collect the ball, instead nonchalantly laying the putter down on the green for his caddie Alistair McLean, and moving swiftly on to the ninth tee. It was only on arrival on the tee that the Scot allowed himself to share a poorly hidden smirk with Westwood, confirming that he, too, had thought the putt an outrageous one to hole.

It brought the match back to all-square, and after the madness of only one of the first seven holes, when just once was a hole halved, the next five were all shared.

Europe regained the lead for only the second time in the match on the 13th but handed the advantage back straight away by bogeying the 14th. On the 16th, however, it seemed that Montgomerie had been uncharacteristically guilty of a woeful error in judgment. Westwood had hit a good driver, leaving Montgomerie with 240 yards to the green on the risk-and-reward Par 5 and, for the second time that day, he decided to go for the green in two. For the second time, he also put a ball into the river. It was a dangerous play from Montgomerie, and one that seemed to hand the initiative to the Americans. Having witnessed his opponent's error, DiMarco still decided to go for the green in two and proceeded to hit a fabulous shot to 15 feet behind the pin. It put the Americans one hole up at a critical juncture.

For the seventh time in eight matches that day, the 18th hole came into play. And, just as Montgomerie would always like it to be, he had centre stage to himself by the time it came to putting on the green that was surrounded by a mesmerised gallery. He sank the final putt of the first day's play for a birdie that turned potential defeat into a halved match. Incredibly, three of the four afternoon foursomes had finished all square. The only win had come from Europe's García and Donald, over the talismanic duo of Woods and Furyk.

· · · ·

On that Friday evening, Woosnam possessed a contented glow. It wasn't arrogance, or anything like it. But his plan of getting all 12 players out into the field straight away had worked a dream. The two sessions finished 2 ½ to 1 ½ which had left Europe with a first day lead of 5-3 in the great scheme of things and seven of the eight matches had finished on the 18th green. Yet, the momentum was well and truly with Europe and Woosie sensed as much.

It had been an incredible first day, the atmosphere unlike any previous Ryder Cup. Those spectators fortunate enough to have secured tickets by stealth or luck or ingenuity, or who just happened to be on the right invite list to one of the corporate hospitality units that seemed to endlessly line the stretch of holes from the 16th tee to the 18th green, had witnessed Europe resume where they had left off at Oakland Hills in 2004, with the upper hand.

Europe had entered the contest as favourites, priced at 4/5, with the bookmakers for the first time in the contest's history and, after the first two sessions of play, had justified that position. Only one US pairing, that of Woods and Furyk, in the morning fourballs, had managed to win. And that victory had come in the very first match.

The difference? 'Obviously, there were a lot of tight matches. We didn't make a lot of putts. That would be the one thing that I would say was the difference between the teams. I felt like our team hit a lot of good putts but didn't make many. The European team definitely made them. They needed to when they had to, [and] we had a couple of loose shots when we needed to have a couple of good shots,' said Lehman after some reflection.

After months and months of preparing for the match, the first day, as Lehman put it, had passed 'like a blur'. Like those spectators who had stood on grassy banks or nabbed seats in the grandstands to watch the drama unfold, Lehman felt, as the sun set on the day, that it was time to catch his breath, and for some reflection. 'It's a pretty fine line out there between zero points, half a point or one point, we didn't really get much going our way,' he said, spending much of that night reliving, in the team room, what had happened during the first day's play. Every time, though, it all came down to the thin line and the hard fact that the Europeans had made the putts when required; and that the Americans hadn't.

Things could hardly have gone much better that day for Woosnam. He hadn't gone into the week intent on playing all 12 of his players on the first day. It had turned out to be something of a masterstroke.

'No, because I think it's difficult to come in with a plan,' he replied when quizzed if it had been a long term strategy to get everyone out into the field as he did. In contrast, Lehman had insisted earlier in the week that he knew exactly who he would play in the foursomes and had stuck religiously to those pairings. Woosnam had only decided on his pairings after the three days of practice, when he encouraged his players to put some money stakes on the line in their matches so that they would add a more serious edge to their play.

Woosnam was a happy captain in a happy team room that Friday night. Having finished his duties with the international media, he returned to his family of golfers. He reminded them that there was a long way to go yet. He reminded them that they had nothing to be scared of. He reminded them that they had taken the initiative. He told them he wanted more of the same.

FIFTEEN

Growing into Giants

LEE WESTWOOD LAY IN HIS sick bed, but knew fully what was at stake when Ian Woosnam phoned him, the week of the BMW International at Munich at the end of August. If it had been any other time, the answer to the request that Europe's Ryder Cup captain put to the player would almost certainly have been a polite, if non-negotiable, 'No.' On that occasion, however, Westwood was aware that would be the wrong answer. Regardless of how much his body was telling him he was too ill to play in the final counting tournament towards qualification, the answer had to be 'Yes.'

If Westwood hadn't shown how badly he wanted to be a part of the Ryder Cup team, Woosie couldn't possibly have considered him as a 'wild card' pick. Ill and all as he was, Westwood, who'd picked up the virus when playing the previous week's WGC-Bridgestone Invitational, made the trip to Munich. He even managed to get on to the fringes of contention, before his body could take no more.

But, over the four days, Westwood showed Woosie enough to merit a captain's pick. It was a selection that had irked Thomas Bjørn, at least at the time. Yet, after his performance in Friday's opening sessions—two appearances that had resulted in one win and one halved match—Westwood's selection not only looked very much the correct one on his captain's part, it smacked of genius.

Westwood had made his debut in the Ryder Cup at Valderrama in 1997, and had been a mainstay ever since. Some people were born to play in such contests, and he proved time and time again that he was one of them. He had always qualified by right, having finished sixth, second, sixth and fifth in the respective qualifying campaigns from 1997 through to the 2004 match in Detroit. But the 2006 season had not been a good one for Westwood, and his failure to qualify automatically for the team meant that it was Woosnam's safety net that rescued him from watching the match at home on television.

Westwood's grandmother had died in March, and the man, who had decided to play mainly on the PGA Tour in the early part of the season, much to the displeasure of Woosnam, found it hard to get over her death. He missed five straight cuts Stateside; a miserable run that had started with the Masters at Augusta. But, once back in Europe, there were sufficiently encouraging performances— fourth in the European Open, second in the Deutsche Bank TPC of Europe—to indicate that his game wasn't too far away from where he wanted it.

Not long after Woosnam made that leap of faith by selecting him as a 'wild card' along with Darren Clarke, ahead of the likes of Bjørn, Ian Poulter and Carl Petterson, Westwood's mother, Trish, was clearing out his grandmother's belongings. Almost five months had passed since Joan Westwood's death. One of the items that caught Westwood's mother's attention was a brooch, designed in the shape of a green shamrock and surrounded by gold. An omen perhaps? She passed it on to her son, and Westwood made a point of putting the newly found lucky charm into a watertight pocket of his Team Europe golf bag throughout the Ryder Cup.

Westwood had gone to bed on Friday night after the first day's endeavours exhausted but happy. It had been a good day's work, which included partnering his friend Clarke to an emotional one hole victory over Phil Mickelson and Chris DiMarco in the fourballs. When he awoke on the Saturday morning, it was to the reality that an even tougher task potentially lay ahead of him and Clarke: the pair had been drawn to play against Tiger Woods and

Jim Furyk in the third of the scheduled four fourball matches of the Ryder Cup's third session.

The weather that Saturday morning was a tad on the nasty side, as a heavy and consistent rain doused the course—once again ensuring that 'lift, clean and place' would be in play—and the conditions made the job tough on the caddies tasked with ensuring that clubs remained dry throughout the deluge.

Undaunted by the weather, the crowds, equipped with rain gear and non-metal spikes (the metal variety failed to make it through the security scanning machines that everyone was submitted to on the way into the course) and plastic-tipped umbrellas had once again flocked to the venue. By the time Paul Casey and Robert Karlsson walked to the first tee for their opening fourball match of the second day with Stewart Cink and JJ Henry, the atmosphere was electric.

Just as they had done on the previous day, the crowds were packed into the grandstand around the first tee, with not a spare seat to be found, and, promoting a carnival atmosphere, the spectators serenaded each player in turn. The Americans were cheered loudly; it was just that the Europeans were cheered louder.

On the Friday, Karlsson and Casey had grabbed an early initiative over the same two Americans only to require a fightback at the end in order to salvage a halved match. Instead of going out in the second match as they had done on the first day, both captains, who had each kept the respective partnerships intact, had gone for the same strategy of promoting the pairs to the top match for the second day. The double manoeuvrings had resulted in Messrs Casey and Karlsson and Messrs Cink and Henry once again going head-to-head in fourballs.

Remarkably, the outcome proved to be as inconclusive as the first time they'd met: a halved match! Although Casey and Karlsson turned two-up, things were a little off-kilter on the home run, prompted by a strategy on the 10th green that went wrong. On the Par 5 hole, Karlsson had put his third shot to just two feet and the Europeans decided that it would be a good thing if the Swede putted out of turn to secure the birdie and to put pressure on the two Americans. Such plans were clever only if they went right, but Karlsson missed the two-footer and Casey then missed his longer birdie effort. When Cink calmly rolled in his birdie, the Americans were back in the ball game at one down.

Henry had proven to be a tough, resolute competitor and he came down strong by the Liffey when the pressure was at its most intense. On the 16th, Henry produced a magnificent second shot over the river to 20 feet and followed up by sinking the eagle putt to take the match level. And, on the 17th, Henry again hit the Europeans in the gut with an iron approach that led to a tap-in birdie, putting the USA one-up going to the 18th. It was the only match that morning to reach the 18th but, just as it had done the previous day, it didn't prove to be America-friendly. Instead, Casey maintained his unbeaten fourball record in the Ryder Cup and rescued a halved match for the home team by boldly sinking a tricky five-footer for birdie.

· · · ·

A tiny piece of Castellón had transported itself to the first tee for the arrival of García and Olazábal for the second fourball match that Saturday. A giant yellow and red Spanish flag was unfurled. García looked at Olazábal and smiled. Phil Mickelson and Chris DiMarco stood just a couple of feet away and the American fans who had infiltrated the grandstand around the tee made some encouraging sounds, just to let them know they were not alone.

García's presence in the European team room had been immense all week. 'He's just a big heap of energy swirling around in the room,' the Swedish 'rookie' Robert Karlsson had remarked of the young Spaniard. As a double act, García and Olazábal thrived in the fourballs and, after just two holes of their match, Mickelson and DiMarco walked off the second green a hole down and convinced that some magical force was at work.

Of all the Americans, DiMarco's demeanour was the one that most mirrored that of García. He had the same Latin temperament, something he attributed to his Italian bloodline, and he didn't need to be encouraged too much by his partner to indulge in some high-fives and fist-pumps when the native New Yorker halved the match with a birdie of his own on the third.

DiMarco's exuberance didn't last as long as he would have liked. On the Par 5 fourth hole, Olazábal's three wood approach from the fairway found a greenside bunker and, with the deftest of touches, he splashed the ball out of the heavy sand to two feet. When he rolled in the birdie, Europe had regained a one hole lead and an initiative they were not to relinquish. The Americans were hit by a birdie blitz around the turn that effectively sealed the match for García and Olazábal.

Whenever García incurred a wayward shot, which was rare, Olazábal provided the back-up. On the eighth, a Par 3 where the flag was positioned perilously close to the Liffey, García's tee shot hugged the river bank. Olazábal rescued his young compatriot by hitting his tee-shot to 15-feet and rolled in the birdie putt.

On the ninth, García's superb iron approach from 184 yards finished five feet behind the pin to set up another birdie that left them three-up as they made the walk to the 10th tee. While Olazábal and García chatted incessantly in their native tongue on the way to the long Par 5, Mickelson and DiMarco were as shell-shocked as children who had arrived at the North Pole only to discover that Santa didn't exist.

With momentum very much on their side, Olazábal was again the European hero on the 10th hole, when he put pressure on DiMarco by holing his birdie putt before the American's effort from closer to the cup missed. Mickelson had been strangely subdued while the Europeans moved farther and farther ahead, but finally secured a birdie for his team on the 14th. It merely reduced the deficit from four to three holes, and time was running out for the Americans.

When the 15th and 16th holes were shared in pars and birdies respectively, all that was left was for García and Olazábal to hug each other on the 16th green. They savoured their 100% partnership from two fourballs matches, and listened to the chants of 'Ole-Ole-Ole' that drifted across to them from the packed grandstands on the other side of the river.

Olazábal's last experience of the Ryder Cup had been at Brookline in 1999 when it had seemed that the world and its mother had run onto the 17th green in his singles match, while the Spaniard still had a birdie putt to keep the match alive, after Justin Leonard holed a raker. On that Saturday at The K Club, with two wins from two in the bag, Olazábal was jokingly asked if he had put a putting curse on the US team.

'I'm not guilty,' he replied, and threw his hands in the air in mock innocence. But he possessed a mischievous grin all the same.

· · · ·

WITH HIS RECENTLY ACQUIRED LUCKY charm tucked into a pocket in the blue and yellow golf bag carried on the shoulders of his caddie, John Graham, or 'Scotchie' as he had become known in the 27 years he had spent in the caddy shack, Westwood retraced the steps he had taken the previous morning with Darren Clarke, from the putting green to the first tee. The journey was no more than 150 yards, but as they walked across the tarmac road, separated from the masses of golf fans by metal barriers, the two men slowed their gait as if to take a deep breath and focus on the encounter that lay ahead with America's 'big two' of Tiger Woods and Jim Furyk.

In their fourball match the previous day, Westwood and Clarke had taken out the other talismanic duo from the United States, Phil Mickelson and Chris DiMarco. While Westwood had teamed-up with Colin Montgomerie in the afternoon foursomes, Clarke had been rested and was eager to get back out onto the golf course. That Woods was in the opposing fourball added to the challenge. Clarke and Woods were great friends, but the Ulsterman was also a fierce competitor and going head-to-head with the world's number one in matchplay constituted a version of golfing nirvana.

Woods had been in irresistible form in tournaments running up to the Ryder Cup. His strokeplay streak from the British Open to the Deutsche Bank championship in Boston had stretched to five wins, and, although his Ryder Cup record in four previous appearances failed to match his individual dominance, Woods had grown into his role as one of the team's on-course leaders. He carried a 1-1-0 record with him onto the tee after the previous day's exertions. It wasn't long before Woods and Furyk realised they were swimming against the tide.

Clarke proved to be the strongman of the European pairing. While Woods was to go through the entire match without procuring a single birdie, Clarke grabbed back-to-back birdies on the fourth and fifth to move his side two-up. On the fourth, he hit a wedge to four feet for birdie and, then, on the fifth, where Woods pushed his drive into the trees, Clarke hit an approach to three feet. Two-up at the turn, Clarke kept up the pressure. On the 11th, playing out of rough, Clarke hit his approach to four feet for another winning birdie. And when Westwood rolled in a 15-footer for birdie on the 14th, it put the Europeans dormie four-up.

There was no great sense of panic from Clarke or Westwood when Furyk responded by holing out from eight feet on the 15th, the first hole either American had won all day. It was to be a short and sweet revival. On the 16th, Clarke showboated by chipping-in from off the back of the green for a birdie that secured a 3 and 2 win. He hardly noticed the rain that belted down as he raised his wedge in salutation to the fans who had erupted in ecstasy on the far side of the river. It was a finish that was the stuff of dreams. Woods shook his hands, looked him in the eye, and said, 'Well done.'

It had been a great morning for Clarke and Westwood. Not so for Woods, who had failed to find the pace of the greens, or Furyk. 'We all have times when we're in sync and out of sync. Just at the minute, Tiger's struggling a little bit with his timing. It happens to us all and I think Tiger's standards are so high, it is just highlighted more whenever he doesn't meet those standards,' said Clarke.

·   ·   ·   ·

ANY TIME LEHMAN PASSED A scoreboard, and there were many of them dotted strategically around the Palmer Course, the sea of blue figures —of Europe, in contrast to the red of the United States—simply confirmed what the delirious roars reverberating everywhere told him: that Europe, not his team, had come out of the stalls fastest that Saturday morning.

But there was one honourable exception to the European dominance. In the bottom fourball match, Lehman had decided that the time had come to give Zach Johnson his Ryder Cup debut. He had paired Johnson, known in the team room as 'Back-to-Back-to-Back Zach' because he had once won three tournaments in a row on the Nationwide Tour, with Scott Verplank, one of the most amiable guys on the US team. That the opposition featured Padraig Harrington, a crowd favourite, and Henrik Stenson, meant that there was a great deal of pressure on the shoulders of Johnson and Verplank.

The previous night Johnson had called Verplank's hotel room when he discovered that the two were to be paired together in the fourballs.

'Hey, dude, we're playing,' he opened. Johnson was delighted to finally get in on some action, before going on to ask Verplank if he'd mind teeing off second. Verplank had been half-asleep when he took the call from this new fourballs partner, but was wide awake when he strode onto the tee with Johnson ahead of Harrington and Stenson. Verplank and Johnson were met with polite applause. The reception given to Harrington and Stenson was raucous.

Verplank edged closer to Johnson and whispered in his ear, 'Zach, this is like the Hawkeyes and we are going to the big house.'

Johnson nodded back,

'This is it, right here. It doesn't get any better than this.'

It was at that point that Verplank noticed that Johnson had a 'little twinkle' in his eye.

'There's nothing like going into somebody else's house and giving them a fight,' Verplank recalled.

It didn't take long for Lehman to discover that Johnson, especially, was not fazed by the huge support that Harrington's every move generated. As the rain pummelled the course, he accumulated more birdies in his round than the three other American fourballs combined in what turned out to be one of the most impressive performances by an individual in the Ryder Cup. Harrington, who had four birdies on his own card, and Stenson, had run into that Saturday morning's form player, and there was very little they could do about it.

Johnson had seven birdies in 17 holes.

'All I did was rub massage oil on his back, give him water and pat his forehead,' said Verplank. By any standards, it constituted a fine morning's work for Johnson who had so impressed Lehman with his hot birdie streak that the US captain promoted him to a place on that afternoon's foursomes, ironically at the expense of Verplank.

• • • •

A PERFECT SYMMETRY HAD ACCOMPANIED Europe's performances in the opening three sessions: each had been won by a margin of 2 ½ to 1 ½, all of which meant that Ian Woosnam's team had established a 7 ½ to 4 ½ advantage when the Saturday morning fourballs finished. If the European team accepted their lot with the cold acceptance that was unique to elite sportsmen, there was a sense of disbelief among the general public who sought to catch their breath by nibbling at one of the public catering areas that had been created on-site for the Ryder Cup.

Little were those European supporters to realise that there were better feats still to materialise on that grey, overcast day when the weather gods contrived to test the patience of a saint with an unpredictable fusion of heavy showers and bright sunshine. And little were those American supporters, who had arrived in Ireland in good numbers, to realise that their team were to slip farther behind as the day progressed.

The US team had brought its share of celebrity supporters. Michael Jordan had followed Woods assiduously, win or lose, while former US President, George Bush Senior, was one of those who continued to fly the flag, quite literally, in encouraging the American team.

At one point on that Saturday afternoon, as the Americans attempted to turn a tide that was getting stronger with each passing minute, Bush—out on the course, wearing a baseball cap emblazoned with the stars and stripes—had approached Corey Pavin, the vice-captain to Tom Lehman.

'Hey Corey, can you get out there and putt for us?' enquired the former President. Pavin, who had been strongly considered for a captain's pick, smiled back. He had won the US Bank Championship in Milwaukee, which gave him more wins on the PGA Tour in 2006 than four of his players, and he was as exasperated as anyone.

Things didn't get any better for the Americans as the foursomes unfolded that Saturday afternoon, and Paul Casey was to be responsible for one of the mightiest noises of all with an audacious deed in the third foursomes match of the fourth session. In all of Ryder Cup history, only four holes-in-one had been recorded before the Englishman aced the 14th hole to close out a win for himself and David Howell over Stewart Cink and Zach Johnson. Johnson could do no wrong that morning in fourballs, but became a victim of the vagaries of the golfing gods when put on the end of a 5 and 4 beating when thrown into the alternate shot format.

The roar that greeted Casey's hole-in-one, the first since Howard Clark at Oak Hill in 1995, was loud and long and incredulous. Fists thumped the air, and the throats of young and old shouted until they could do so no longer, until finally the drone of the omnipresent helicopters overhead, which had been blocked out by the vocal homage to Casey's deed, returned.

Before he had taken his shot, Casey and partner David Howell had walked onto the 14th tee with a dormie five-hole lead, and Casey's spectacular finish provided one of the snapshot moments of the 2006 Ryder Cup.

When Casey and Howell had walked from the 12th green to the 13th tee, their captain Ian Woosnam had appeared. He imparted the information that players were using three-irons off the tee on the next short hole, the 14th. Casey had nodded, storing the titbit in his head. But when it came time to play his tee shot on the short hole, Casey reached into his bag and retrieved a four-iron. He knew that the adrenalin was pumping through his body, so near were they to securing a win, and felt that a three-iron represented too much club.

From the time that Casey launched his four-iron tee shot, he knew it was good.

'It was an absolute flush of a four-iron for Paul. It was beautiful, never anywhere other than close. For the ball to drop in was surreal,' said Howell. Just how good it was, was acknowledged by the roar that greeted the ball landing just a few feet short of the hole and dutifully following the perfect path into the tin cup. Casey didn't see the ball drop, but knew instinctively what had happened by the acclaim coming back from greenside. He threw the club into the air in sheer joy and, then, conceded a hole-in-one to Cink and Johnson who were not required to play their tee-shot.

As if doubting what he had achieved, Casey turned to the Jumbotron television screen positioned between the 14th tee and the 13th green. He watched without blinking for fear that it was a dream, and, in the action replay, he watched as the ball rolled into the hole. Just as had occurred in real time, the crowds again erupted.

'It was a very surreal situation, not actually walking up to a green and putting our or shaking hands. A fantastic moment,' he recalled.

Casey's caddie, Craig Connelly, had worked two Solheim Cups with Trish Johnson and Iben Tinning but had never experienced a two-week run like the one he now found himself in. Casey might have won the World Matchplay in Wentworth the previous week and claimed a first prize of £1 million, but the hole-in-one to close out a Ryder Cup match was simply priceless. Connelly didn't mind in the least when he was asked to walk the 210 yards to the hole to retrieve the golf ball.

'I've had many holes in one, but never in a tournament round of golf, let alone in a big situation like this ... and especially to close out a match. You know, it's just probably something that will go down in history,' said Casey.

Nobody in the history of the Ryder Cup had ever performed a hole-in-one to match that of Casey's. Peter Butler's at Muirfield in 1973, Nick Faldo's at the Belfry in 1993, Costantino Rocca's at Oak Hill in 1995, Howard Clark's at Oak Hill in 1995; none of them had been to close out a match. None of them had the consequence of turning to an opponent on the tee and conceding their shot to them. Casey did.

· · · ·

EUROPE WON THE SECOND AFTERNOON's foursomes by a margin of 2 ½ to 1 ½, the same score as they had taken in the first three sessions. 10-6. Who could have envisaged it? Casey stole the show with his ace on the 14th to partner David Howell to victory over Zach Johnson and Stewart Cink but Europe's dominance, which had Tom Lehman ashen-faced by Saturday evening, owed more to just luck, which was how any hole-in-one should be construed.

When Europe had upset the odds to defeat the United States in the 2002 Ryder Cup at The Belfry, a match that had been delayed for 12 months due to the atrocities of 9/11, the team's captain, Sam Torrance, had remarked that, 'Out of the shadows come heroes.' Woosnam's problem, if it could be called that, was that every one of his team had stood up to the Americans. His team showed a hunger that was at odds with the fact that they'd won the previous two Ryder Cups.

Nobody epitomised Europe's desire greater than Sergio García. He was the joker in the team room. But he was more than that. The spotty faced kid who had first played in the Ryder Cup in 1999 had matured into a player who revelled in assuming responsibility. On that Saturday afternoon, he again teamed up with Luke Donald who, day by day, had come more and more out of his shell. Off the course, more often than not, García was the guy by his side forever talking and Donald forever listening.

Their real bond was golf. García and Donald were the two highest ranked players in the world on the European team. Donald had been a little hurt when omitted from the first day's fourballs, but took it on the chin. When he was again omitted from the second day's fourballs, he again took it on the chin. His response was to form an imposing partnership with García and, having accounted for Tiger Woods and Jim Furyk on day one, their next foursomes victims were Phil Mickelson and David Toms.

The 2006 Ryder Cup had turned into a disaster for Mickelson. It would prove to be his last golf commitment for the year. When it was done and dusted, Lefty felt his time would be better spent devoted to his family than playing golf. But Mickelson badly wanted to win that foursomes. His much-heralded partnership with Chris DiMarco, which had its genesis in the previous year's President's Cup, had imploded. After one half-point from three matches, Lehman felt the need for change that paired Mickelson with Toms.

They were never at the races. Donald made the decisive blow when he holed a long birdie putt on the 16th. It was a win that gave the Donald-García foursomes partnership a fourth straight win, going back to Oakland Hills in 1995 where they had first played together.

As far as García was concerned, the methodology for their success was a simple one.

'We just make a really good couple ... he just hits the drives, hits the ball down the middle, and I somehow get it around the hole and he just taps it in. It works perfect.'

. . . .

Vaughn Taylor had waited longer than any player to make his Ryder Cup debut. For one and a half days, he had been cast in a supporting role and joined the wives and girlfriends tagging along the fairways behind one match or another. His chance to play finally arrived in the second series of foursomes, which at least ensured that he had played a match before the final day's singles.

'I think I sat the longest because I think I was a little rusty. I wasn't quite hitting it as well (in practice) as I wanted to. I just had to support the team and, when I finally got my chance, I had to try making something out of it,' he said.

Chad Campbell was tasked with nursing Taylor for a debut against two of the toughest cookies in the European camp: Lee Westwood and Colin Montgomerie. Taylor, in actual fact, didn't need any minding. He was well capable of fending for himself, going toe-to-toe with the two European heavyweights.

'I had a blast,' said Taylor, who secured a half-point after a tough old encounter. The critical moment came on the 17th, where Monty played a weak chip from greenside rough and left Westwood with an eight-footer for par which he missed.

· · · ·

THE SOLE AMERICAN WIN OF the foursomes came from Tiger Woods and Jim Furyk. No two men had lived under so much pressure in the run-up to the match as Padraig Harrington and Paul McGinley. On television ads and advertising billboards all around Ireland, the voices and faces of the pair encapsulated just what playing host to the great match entailed to the country.

Nothing would have given the two Dubliners greater pleasure than to repeat their feat from Oakland Hills two years previously when, to the sounds of Molly Malone being sung around the suburbs of Detroit, they had beaten Woods and Furyk. There was no repeat. In a high-quality match, where the tone was set with birdies on the third, the USA pairing moved ahead on the Par 5 fourth hole when Furyk rolled in his eight-footer for birdie and McGinley missed his attempt from a similar distance. On the fifth, the two Irishman fell a further hole behind after McGinley's drive hit trees down the left and finished in thick rough.

It was not until the eighth hole, tight by the Liffey, that the huge galleries got a chance to truly cheer on their favoured sons. Harrington hit a six-iron over the pin and McGinley sank the birdie putt to reduce the margin to one. Their joy was to be short-lived. Harrington's approach to the ninth missed the green and they were unable to get up and down for par. So it was that Woods and Furyk walked to the 10th tee two-up and very much in control of their own destiny.

But Harrington and McGinley refused to lie down. On the 11th, McGinley holed a 12-footer for birdie only for Furyk to follow him in. Hole halved. On the 12th, Harrington's tee-shot finished no more than two feet from the hole and McGinley stepped up to hole the birdie and again reduce the margin to one. Yet again, however, the Irish were to do themselves no favours on the next hole, where Harrington's approach found a greenside bunker from which they failed—unlike the Americans—to get up and down to save par.

Two up playing the 15th, the Americans put a dagger into Irish hearts. Woods came up short of the flag with his approach, while Harrington set up McGinley for a feasible birdie attempt. Furyk sank his 40-foot birdie putt, McGinley's lipped out. Three up with three to play, the match finished tamely on the 16th, where McGinley attempted to reach the green in two from semi-rough, only to catch his shot heavy. The ball plunged, along with their hopes, into the river.

'We're obviously disappointed to lose, but the bottom line is that we played the number one and number two in the world, both of them on their game,' said McGinley, 'and when you do that, you're going to have a tough day. And we did. We battled well. We fought hard, but one and two in the world on their game is a pretty formidable combination.'

If there was solace for the Irish pairing, it came in the overall team situation. Europe headed into the final of singles with a 10-6 lead. The odds were stacked in their favour.

. . . .

THOSE SPECTATORS WHO HAD TICKETS hanging in plastic pouches from around their necks lingered as long as they could that Saturday evening. They wanted to remain, so that some of the magic that hung in the gathering dusk could be captured and kept. Only one of the four foursomes matches had reached the 18th green, with its grand amphitheatre of mounding and a clubhouse that had grown in size out of necessity over the years, but it had been another exhilarating day's play.

'Where were you, granddad, mother, brother, when Paul Casey holed his four-iron?' Some 45,000 spectators had walked through the gates into The K Club that Saturday morning and the same number had left in the evening, abuzz with excitement for what had happened that day and abuzz with anticipation for what lay ahead the following day. To be sure, many of them had witnessed Casey's dream shot in the flesh. To be sure, most had only heard the shouts and saw, like the player himself, the actual shot on one of the nine Jumbotron television screens located around the course.

That evening, Ian Woosnam and Tom Lehman attempted to make sense of what had unfolded over two days of fourballs and foursomes. Solomon himself would have struggled. The simple fact stated that nine of the 16 matches had made it to the 'Hooker's Graveyard,' otherwise known as the Par 5 18th hole on the Palmer Course. The results would forever show that Europe had won two of those matches that went to the death, that the United States had won one, and that six of them had been halved.

Yet, despite the fact that any of those matches could have gone either way, a rub of the green there or a bounce of the ball here,

Europe had managed to establish a 10-6 lead overall going into Sunday's 12 singles. Poor Lehman, who had done almost everything right in the months and weeks and days leading up to the actual match, must have wondered why the golfing gods had spurned him and his team.

The kernel of the problem, Lehman decided, was that the Europeans were holing putts. His team weren't. Simple.

'My team has been hitting a lot of good putts, they're just not going in. I saw a lot of putts that looked beautiful (but didn't drop),' he explained. The one that was freshest in Lehman's memory was that of Chad Campbell, who had featured in the only foursomes to make it to the 18th. Lehman was right. Campbell's putt to win grazed the hole, but refused to drop.

In troubled times, with his back and those of his team against the wall, it was natural that Lehman should reach into the past for inspiration. Brookline in 1999 came to mind.

'I feel like tomorrow could be the day. A lot of guys are hitting putts that look really, really good and they are just not going in the hole. When (putts) start going in, they go in, in buckets.'

His attitude was remarkably similar to that conveyed by Ben Crenshaw, who had been in a similar position going into the singles seven years earlier. On the Saturday night of the 1999 Ryder Cup match at the Country Club in Brookline, the United States team captain Ben Crenshaw had ushered his friend, George W Bush, into the team room. It wasn't a particularly happy room. After two days of play, and with only the singles remaining, the Europeans held a 10-6 lead that had the home team, without a win since 1993, facing the prospect of a third successive defeat.

Prior to leaving the course that Saturday, Crenshaw had insisted that he hadn't given up hope of an American revival.

'I'm a big believer in fate, I have a good feeling about this,' Crenshaw said. 'That's all I am going to tell you.'

Bringing the future President of the United States into the US team room was Crenshaw's trump card, a ploy to galvanise his men. Bush recited the letter from William Barret Travis to 'To the People of Texas and All Americans in the World.' Travis was the commander of the small Texas force that held off, but was ultimately wiped out by the Mexican army at the Battle of the Alamo in 1836 when Texas was fighting to become an independent republic.

In the letter, Travis wrote: 'I have sustained a continual bombardment and cannonade for 24 hours and have not lost a man. The enemy has demanded surrender at discretion, otherwise the garrison are to be put to the sword, if the fort is taken. I have answered the demand with a cannon shot, and our flag still waves proudly from the walls. I shall never surrender or retreat. VICTORY OR DEATH.'

These were the words that Bush spoke to Crenshaw's team.

Lehman had been in the US team room that night when the future President spoke. The following day, he went out, at number one in the singles order, and beat Lee Westwood. His win was the catalyst for the most remarkable comeback in Ryder Cup history. From 6-10 down, the United States, much to the delight of the frenzied crowds, staged a fightback that ultimately saw them regain the Ryder Cup on a 14 ½ to 13 ½ score line.

Could lightning strike twice? Lehman knew that his team faced a tougher task on foreign soil.

'I know that our team has a chance, and I know that we have the ability to get the job done, and I know that our guys are determined to do it. So, do I have a feeling? I have a feeling that our team is going to play incredibly inspired golf. They are going to go out and, no matter who they are playing against, they are going to lay it on the line. They are going to give it all that they have got.'

That day, watching the foursomes, Woosnam and his friend David J Russell were in the European captain's Club Car. As they moved from one match to another, keeping in touch with Des Smyth and Peter Baker by walkie talkie communications, Woosie pulled the electric buggy to a halt and pointed to one of the large scoreboards.

'How would you feel if it was all red?' Woosnam asked. At the time, the board was a sea of blue and the question was asked simply for the sake of asking, to convey to his pal that golf was a game that could change as quickly as the Irish weather, that golf was by its nature unpredictable.

But Woosnam recalled the incident with Russell later that evening as he contemplated taking a 10-6 lead into the final day's singles. His team had the chance to be a part of history, to be the first European team to win the Ryder Cup for a third successive time.

'You know, anything can happen very quickly in this game,' reiterated Woosnam. His men would hear that mantra all evening in the team room. The Welshman was determined there would be no fear of complacency.

Woosnam was preaching to the converted as he repeated his warning about the need for the team to be on their guard.

'By no means are we finished yet,' said a wary Paul McGinley on the Saturday evening. 'We've got a long way to go tomorrow.'

García had been Europe's star performer over the first two days. With a 100% record from four matches, he had shown, yet again, that he could raise his game for the Ryder Cup. 'We don't want to go out there thinking, oh, let's get four and a half points. That's not the way to go. We want to go out there, try to win the singles and get as many points as we can. That's the main goal, and that's what we have to do. It's simple.'

Simple plan or not, Europe had to go out into the singles and put that plan into action.

And what of Woosie's role? 'He might be a short man, but he's got a huge heart and he's been just awesome,' said García.

'Yes, you're right, he is a short man. There's no question about that Sergio,' added Montgomerie. 'He is a short man with a very, very big heart.'

'But I think he has grown three inches this week.'

'You're right. I think he has grown. He is taller.'

Woosnam had indeed grown in stature as the week had gone on, just as his team had done.

SIXTEEN

Destiny, Destiny

Co. Kildare, Ireland. Sunday, 24 September, 2006.

MEMORIES! TEARS! BEERS! CHEERS! ACES! Birdies! Bogeys, of the golfing kind! Bogeys, of a different champagne-induced kind (out of Ian Woosnam's nose)! Yuck! In the dark of early morning on that Sunday, they had started to make the final pilgrimage. It rained, but the contingency plan to drag the 36th Ryder Cup into another extra day, a Monday, wasn't needed and those dedicated followers of golf, all 45,000 of them, who moved into position early for the final enactment did so with a sense of purpose and a belief that something special lay in store. What memories would be forever stored in their heads by day's end?

For those fans draped in ponchos or smothered in wet gear, those fans who ignored the rain as they trooped into the The K Club that Sunday morning, it was pretty much official: Woosnam was a mastermind, not the 'pathetic' captain that the spurned Thomas Bjørn had mistakenly predicted just a fortnight before the greatest golf show on earth. He would not need a back door to escape the country. For the previous two days, of foursomes and fourballs, Woosie's European team—who, for the first time in Ryder Cup history had carried the responsibility of favourites into golf's greatest team tournament—had outplayed the United States, and the time for deliverance had arrived.

Europe carried a 10-6 lead into the final day of 12 singles and, just as he had done at Oakland Hills in 2004, Colin Montgomerie had been tasked with leading from the front. In the second singles, Sergio García's named had been pencilled in.

'Monty's a very quick player. He likes to get out there. Sergio is pretty quick. We wanted to let them get out there, to play their own game,' explained Woosnam. He hadn't fooled anyone. Montgomerie and García were his leaders. He wanted them to lead. If the Americans were to stage a fightback, it would be the hard way.

Woosnam had sought to keep any hint of complacency out of the team room on the Saturday night. Yet, as each and every player assessed the singles pairings over dinner on that penultimate night of a little wining and lots of dining, nobody managed to escape the thought that, maybe, their captain had attempted to manipulate the order so that one man in particular could deliver.

Darren Clarke, who had shown incredible resolve in playing and competing so soon after his wife's death, had been positioned in the seventh singles against Zach Johnson. If Woosie's game plan worked out, Clarke's match, if he won, would be there or thereabouts when victory was determined. If!

As the clock ticked towards five minutes past 11am, Montgomerie completed the last actions of his pre-round practice. He had ten minutes to kill. The Scot, a mainstay of Team Europe, had always thrived in the white-hot environment of the Ryder Cup, the white-knuckle ride of world golf, and he finished his routine with a couple of short putts on the practice green before he headed towards the first tee. As he made his way across the avenue, those spectators who lined the way raised the volume levels and the noise transferred itself to those in the packed grandstand that curled around the tee box.

Montgomerie thought he had seen and heard everything in the seven previous Ryder Cups he had played in. He was wrong. The shouts on that first tee started out simply as 'Monty, Monty' but, suddenly, changed track. Instead, the crowds—mainly Irish, but with a healthy smattering of English and Scottish and Welsh and Spanish and Swedish—serenaded him to the air of '*La donna è mobile*' from Rigoletto. As one, they sang:

'Col-in-Mont-gom-e-rie ...

Col-in-Mont-gom-e-rie ...

Col-in-Mont-gom-e-rie ...

Col-in-Mont-gom-e-rie,' a tune, sung *ad nauseam*, that had accompanied the Italian soccer player Paolo Di Canio on his travels around various football grounds.

As Monty strode from the tee box having hit the first drive in his singles match against David Toms, and the first shot in Europe's final day's quest for a place in the history books, he suddenly stopped, turned to salute the crowd by raising his hand, and gave them a shake of the head as only he could. It signalled his appreciation for such a heart-felt send-off. The big man was genuinely touched.

The crowds were to be a huge part of that final day. Those packed around the first tee applauded the American players into the arena and serenaded the Europeans. García and, later, José María Olazábal were given the traditional 'Olé, Olé, Olé' treatment. Luke Donald got his own personal salutation, a guttural yet addictive chorus of 'L-u-u-u-u-u-u-u-u-u-u-k-e.' Luke, a.k.a. Skywalker, loved it. Paul McGinley and Padraig Harrington in turn stood on the tee to renditions of 'Molly Malone.' Others made do with their surnames being shouted out as if from terraces at a soccer ground. 'That reception on the first tee was unbelievable, I think it made us all shake,' said Donald.

There was added gusto, an increase in the noise decibel level if that were possible, to the acclaim that greeted Clarke. To a man and woman, everyone in the stands rose to award him a standing ovation and his opponent, Johnson, warned what to expect, later remarked, 'I expected it to be loud, but it was like a football stadium crowd of 80,000 massed around one tee box. It was pretty remarkable. I felt like I was the away team, playing for the world championship, or something, in another sport.'

The singles order for that final day's play had been decided the previous night, when the respective captains had placed their men in order from one to 12. Tom Lehman had opted to place heavy hitters at the top end and towards the bottom, with his four rookies bunched together in the middle. The US captain decided on an order of David Toms, Stewart Cink, Jim Furyk, Tiger Woods, Chad Campbell, JJ Henry, Zach Johnson, Vaughn Taylor, Brett Wetterich, Phil Mickelson, Chris DiMarco, and finally Scott Verplank. Woosnam's order brought a sequence of Colin Montgomerie, Sergio García, Paul Casey, Robert Karlsson, Luke Donald, Paul McGinley, Darren Clarke, Henrik Stenson, David Howell, José María Olazábal, Lee Westwood, and finally Padraig Harrington.

If the Americans were to have any chance of quietening the crowds, they needed to put some red figures on the giant scoreboards as they had done in the 1999 Ryder Cup match at Brookline. And, Cink, a captain's pick, achieved that in the second singles against García. The Spaniard had been Europe's dynamo, both in the team room and on the course, all week; but he ran into a train when he went up against Cink. García's 100% record was reduced to an 80% return. Any American player would have given his bottom dollar for the same!

Cink started birdie-birdie-par-birdie-birdie—the best golf played by anyone on that final day of singles—and by the time they walked off the seventh green, the American, incredibly, had moved five holes up on Europe's highest-ranked player. García tried to fight his way back into the match. He won the short eighth, after Cink found the river off the tee, and further reduced the deficit—to three holes—when he made a 10-foot birdie to claim the 11th.

García felt that the momentum had suddenly been transferred to him, but he was wrong. Cink holed a 60-foot birdie putt on the 12th and, crestfallen, García's effort from 15-feet failed to find the hole. Cink had moved four-up again, and would not lose another hole. Fittingly, the match ended in the style that it had started: García chipped-in for birdie on the 15th from just off the fringe of the green, only to be followed in by Cink who holed from 20 feet.

It was put to García that Cink had a hot putter.

'No, I don't think he had a hot putter. I think his putter melted! It must have melted. I've never seen anything like it ... when I got to five (down), I thought, well, should I make this short and go help my partners? Or, should I at least try to get a bit farther down the road? So, I saw Woosie on (number) eight and he gave me a fist pump and a bit of a charge ... and then Stewart holes a 60-footer on me on 12, a 40-footer on the next and I have to make a 20-footer to halve and, then, on 15, I chip in and he rolls in a 20-footer. So, thank you very much, see you in two years.'

His match finished early, all García could do was to retreat back to act as cheerleader for his team-mates. He was to prove darn good in that role, too. So too was his girlfriend, Morgan Norman, daughter of the Great White Shark.

Tiger Woods also did his captain's bidding. The world's number one was pitted against the 6-feet 5-inch Swede, Robert Karlsson, in the fourth singles match and, although Karlsson threw down the gauntlet by birdying the opening hole, Woods, back in control of his own destiny and playing his own ball, took charge and even managed to overcome a rather bizarre incident on the seventh hole that left him without a nine-iron for the remainder of his round.

Woods had moved one-up as he stood by the water's edge on the seventh green—a hole known as 'Michael's Favourite,' so-named by The K Club's co-owner Dr Smurfit—when a strange thing happened. Rather nonchalantly, Woods handed the nine-iron that he had used for his approach shot to his caddie, Steve Williams. It was not to be a moment that Williams would cherish. The bagman slipped as he took hold of the club and, putting his hand out to stop from falling, let the iron and the towel he was holding drop into the lake. While the towel floated long enough for Williams to retrieve it, the club had no such buoyancy. It sank to the bottom of the lake.

What could Tiger do but laugh? Williams didn't know whether to laugh or cry.

'That was interesting,' recalled Woods. 'I handed my ball to Stevie to have it cleaned and he was going to rinse the nine-iron in the water. He sure did that all right. He slipped on the rock and it was either him or the nine-iron, so he chose (to let go) the nine-iron.' A wet-suited frogman eventually retrieved the club from the bottom of the lake, but Woods had reached the 15th hole—and pretty much finished the job—by the time it was put back in his bag.

Woods, again watched by his friend Michael Jordan, who had been a constant presence throughout the Ryder Cup, managed just fine without his missing club and finished out the match for a 3 and 2 win that gave him three points from a possible five. It constituted his best-ever return in a Ryder Cup and he emerged as the leading US point scorer in the match. But it hadn't been enough, and the domino effect that Lehman had looked for from the top-order of players failed to materialise.

In fact, only three Americans—Cink, Woods and Verplank in the bottom singles—managed to win, while JJ Henry was awarded a generous halved match by Paul McGinley when an attention-seeking streaker interrupted their match on the 18th green. For the most part, the scoreboards were awash with blue numbers that indicated Europe's supremacy. It had been a familiar tale from the first morning's fourballs on Friday morning, and a trend that had continued throughout the match.

The first European point that Sunday was put up by Montgomerie. After his great send-off from the first tee, Monty had gotten down to business quickly, winning the third and fourth holes birdies to go two-up on Toms. He was never in danger, yet still had to play the 18th—for the fourth time in four matches—before he got up and down from a greenside bunker for a birdie that halved the hole and secured the win.

'Ian thought it was good I went out first. I'm probably the quickest player on the team and it was important that I got off to a good start and got some blue on the board early, which I did,' said the Scot.

Paul Casey had been pitted against Jim Furyk, but it was a time in his life when he could do no wrong. A day earlier, he had closed out his foursomes match with a hole-in-one on the 14th and, when he arrived on the same tee in his singles with Furyk, he was three-up and in complete control. Lightning rarely strikes twice but, when Casey struck his tee shot on the short hole, he allowed himself a long, lingering look at the ball's flight. He determined before it even touched the putting surface that it would not be a repeat ace.

Casey had birdied four of the first six holes to turn four-up on Furyk, and he eventually finished the one-sided duel with a handshake on the 17th green. Furyk, never a man to quit, had fought back on the homeward run when he won the 11th in birdie and the 16th in eagle. But time had not been on his side. Casey shook hands with Furyk at 3.16pm. Europe had moved into a 12-8 lead. And Casey made his way back the way he had come, to catch up with the developments behind him.

The golf buggy that took Casey back down the 17th hole that curled its way around a bend in the Liffey edged ever closer to the noisiest gathering of all, the huge crowds that had gathered in the grandstands and by the banks of the river on the 16th hole. Thousands of other spectators stood on the walkways fronting the massive corporate hospitality units that lined the fairway. It was an incredible scene.

• • • •

SOME 600 HELICOPTER DROPS A day had taken place during the Ryder Cup; dynamic evidence, if it were needed, of the roaring Celtic Tiger economy that had benefited Ireland in a decade of huge growth, and which was highlighted further by the fact that the match had finally reached an island with one third of the world's links courses and a rich history in the tournament. Tommy O'Keeffe and his son, Jonathan, were among the crowds down by the 16th hole as Europe edged closer and closer to victory. But O'Keeffe, like the vast majority of those urging on Europe's win, had arrived at the venue by a more orthodox route.

He owned a barber shop and unisex hairdressers in Edenmore, in the suburbs on the north side of Dublin, and had been one of over 100,000 people who entered the worldwide random lottery for tickets on the European Tour's website. The odds were against him getting a ticket, but he had registered his credit card details looking for two tickets for the singles on the Sunday and kept his fingers crossed. That had been in May, 2005. Five months later, in October, he got an email back congratulating him on his success in the lottery. Two tickets, as requested.

Two weeks before the match, DHL delivered his prized tickets. With the tickets were strict instructions that they weren't to be sold on. There was no chance of that. This was a dream fulfilled. An avid golfer, and a member of Skerries Golf Club for 27 years, O'Keeffe couldn't believe his luck as he found himself in the thick of the action that Sunday. He assiduously found time for golf, organising outings with friends and ensuring that golf didn't simply revolve around playing his home club. He loved getting up close and personal, watching the professionals at the Irish Open and the European Open, the two European Tour stops in Ireland each year.

He'd been fortunate enough to play the Palmer Course a number of times. The last time he had played, O'Keeffe had lost two new ProVs in the Liffey in foolishly attempting to reach the 16th in two. Once upon a time, he and his friends had even sneaked onto the back tees, those championship markers used in the European Open, and it gave him a new respect for the game that the professionals played.

'Just the power that they put into the swing, it's unreal. If I was to hit a ball like Tiger Woods, I'd have to go straight down to the chiropractors. They all hit it so far. I mean, 186 yards for an eight-iron? There's no doubt, they are a different animal,' said O'Keeffe.

That morning, the two O'Keeffes, father and son, had left their home in Swords and drove to the public park-and-ride facility at Weston Aerodrome in Leixlip. From there, they got the shuttle bus to the course. The procedure had worked seamlessly. They were at the first tee at 10.15am, an hour before Monty's singles match. They found a place halfway down the fairway in the vicinity of where the tee shots would land and, later, they moved around, spending much of the first couple of hours following Tiger, getting to within four or five feet of the great one, and marvelling at what they saw.

On the 12th hole, a Par 3 to a green with water on the left, the two golf fans had a perfect spot, positioned between the green and the tee. They could see players driving off the 11th tee, and the tee shots and putts (or chips) on the short hole. It was a great location. At one point, his son nudged O'Keeffe. Jonathan discreetly pointed at a big, tall, blonde man who stood not too far away from them.

'Do you know who that is?'

'No,' replied Tommy, 'but he looks familiar.'

'That's Boris Becker.'

'No way.'

'Yes way.'

Bold as brass, but unsure if his leg was being pulled, O'Keeffe ventured up to the man who looked like the tennis legend.

'Are you Boris Becker?' he asked.

'I am,' said the German. 'Who are you?'

'I'm Tommy. Delighted to meet you.'

Tommy the Barber had mixed with the great and the good at The K Club, but the scenes over the finishing few holes, especially at the 16th, were ones that would be stored in his head forever more. What's more, he watched and he learned. A couple of weeks later he would play in a seniors open competition at The Island Golf Club. He won, and was cut two shots off his handicap. From 14 down to 12. He attributed it to the inspirational effect of watching the world's greatest players that Sunday.

.   .   .   .

DAVID HOWELL NEVER GOT AS far as the 16th—which had become the principal gathering point—in his singles with Brett Wetterich that Sunday. Wetterich had impressed in the US team's reconnaissance trip to The K Club prior to the match and had also impressed in the practice days, but, as he discovered, there was a massive difference between practice and actually playing in a competition like the Ryder Cup.

In his only outing before the singles, Wetterich (and his fourballs partner Toms) had been caught up in the spell cast by the 'Spanish Armada' on Friday morning. It had been a morning when nothing went right for Wetterich, not even on the rare occasion that he attempted to high-five Toms, but, rather cruelly, Wetterich again found himself in the middle of something extraordinary that Sunday.

Howell and Wetterich had been involved in a close match up to the time that they walked on to the 11th tee. The Englishman was one-up on the American at that stage but then produced a run of birdie-birdie-birdie-birdie to win the following four holes and claim the match by 5 and 4. Howell and Wetterich hugged in a warm and genuine embrace on the 14th green. It was 3.40pm, and Howell's victory had moved Europe into a 13-8 lead.

Europe only needed one more point to retain the trophy as defending champions, and another half-point after that for outright victory and an historic third successive win. It was a matter of when, not if. A tidal wave of inevitability had swept over the singles and the blue numbers on the scoreboards showed that there would be only one winner.

Luke Donald guaranteed the retention of the trophy for Europe when he beat Chad Campbell by a 2 and 1 margin. Europe 14, USA 8. It was a match that emphasised the wicked vagaries of golf. Donald and Campbell had recorded nine straight pars apiece to turn all-square, only for Donald to get hot and Campbell to not. The critical holes were the 11th, 12th and 13th, where Donald went birdie-par-birdie to Campbell's bogey-double bogey-double bogey.

It was revenge of sorts for Donald. Two years previously, in Oakland Hills, Campbell had beaten him quite comfortably.

'It wasn't really about revenge,' insisted Donald though. 'To be honest, our main aim was to win the singles. We had won every other session, the fourballs, the foursomes, both days. We wanted to go out there and just pretend that we weren't trying to get to just 14 and a half [points], we were going to get as many as we could.'

The clock had nudged its way to 3.45pm when Donald finished off Campbell. One minute later—at 3.46pm—Sweden's Henrik Stenson, the 'special one' as Paul Broadhurst had called him early in the season, sealed the deal. Europe 15, USA 8. Stenson's 4 and 3 win over Vaughn Taylor was the moment that Europe were guaranteed victory in the 2006 Ryder Cup and, with virtually every spectator all over the course hearing the news simultaneously on the transistor radios, a simultaneous roar of approval, and not just from those around the 15th green, greeted Stenson's deed.

Stenson had secured an epic win for Europe, an unprecedented third successive victory in the competition following on from the Belfry, near Birmingham, in England in 2002 and Oakland Hills, in Detroit, in 2004. Stenson had trailed early on in his match to Taylor. One down after five holes, Stenson won the sixth with a conceded birdie—after Taylor had been in all sorts of trouble and ran up a double bogey six—and went ahead on the seventh with another birdie. Slowly, but surely, the Swede edged farther and farther ahead. Two-up after nine. Three-up after 12. Four-up after 14.

Shortly before he lined up a seven foot putt on the 15th, Stenson heard another loud roar from up ahead. He suspected that it marked the confirmation of another European victory. He didn't know that it was hailing Donald's accomplishment in ensuring that Europe had retained the trophy. He didn't know that his putt was to win the darn thing. He truly didn't realise the significance of what he was about to do when, with ice cold nerves and a red hot putter, he stroked the par putt into the hole to win his match.

Stenson raised his putter to the skies in triumph. He wanted this moment to go on and on, and he wanted to soak up the acclaim of the crowd. Then, someone told him what he'd done. It was only then that Stenson realised that his putt would go down in history as the one that had won the Ryder Cup in 2006 for Europe. His first reaction, however, was to jump into a cart—issuing high-fives to spectators along the way—as he sought to catch up on Darren Clarke's match ahead.

At 3.55pm, Clarke won his match with Zach Johnson on the 16th green. Europe 16, USA 8. Woosie had so nearly got it right. If Stenson's putt had won the Cup, Clarke's finish provided the raw emotion. It gave Europe deliverance. The Irishman had ridden a roller-coaster of sentiment, yet somehow had kept his resolve to impart one superb shot after another in the three matches that he played. Each match, each outing, had resulted in a win. Victory achieved, he let it all go.

Six weeks to the day after his wife, Heather, had died, Clarke's singles victory prompted an outpouring of emotions. Tears welled in his eyes as his faithful caddie, Billy Foster, gave him a shoulder to cry on and Woosnam was the first to raise Clarke's hands aloft.

'Destiny, destiny,' whispered Woosnam into Clarke's ears.

US captain Tom Lehman wasn't far behind. 'You hurt us real bad. But you know what? We're so glad you were on this team and we're behind you 100%,' Lehman told him.

Clarke and Johnson had played their approach shots to the 16th green, the man from Dungannon three-up at that point, when the ropes that had kept the spectators off the fairway and away from the riverbank came down. The spectators flooded onto the fairway, anticipating and expecting, and crossed towards the river bank to be closer to the action. Clarke delivered. With misty eyes, he looked across the river to where the crowds stood to acclaim him and the roars that came back across that stretch of waterway told him that his people knew and understood and cared.

His singles win crossed team boundaries; Woods, DiMarco, Mickelson, Cink, all came on to the green, because it seemed the right thing to do, and all of them hugged him. Then his own embraced him; García, Casey, Donald, Stenson. One by one, they came to him and held him.

Clarke determined that his golf had been just 'okay', but he was a lone critic. To everyone else, he had performed miraculously well. Not just in his singles, but in the two fourballs wins as well. Before his round, Woosnam had warned him not to look at scoreboards. Clarke hadn't resisted the temptation.

'Sorry, Woosie, but I was looking at the board a little bit. I found it very difficult to not get ahead of myself and keep my emotions in check whenever it was obvious it could come down to my putt. I lost myself a few times out there, but I managed to keep on going and do what I had to do.'

What had the week meant?

'I've got too many memories to list. This week has done a lot for me. It's shown me that a lot of people cared about me and a lot of people cared about Heather. It was very, very touching,' said Clarke.

From that first tee shot on the first hole, Clarke had separated his emotions from his golf. He concentrated on every shot and his first birdie of that glorious day was a winning one, on the fourth. It put Clarke one-up on Johnson. The American birdied to the fifth to go all square, but that was as good as it got for Johnson. When he bogeyed the sixth, it put Clarke ahead again and, by the time they walked off the seventh green, the big Ulsterman had moved two clear. When he birdied the 10th, it put him three holes ahead.

The best had still to come. On the 12th hole, a Par 3, Clarke missed the green with his approach shot. He was four feet off the putting surface and some 40 yards from the hole. He took the putter from Foster, took aim, fired … and watched as the ball, like a missile, stayed true to its line and fell into the hole for an outrageous birdie. The crowds had gone wild for less. Clarke's birdie sent them into ecstasy.

Johnson, game as ever, reduced the deficit by winning the 13th in par. But it wasn't enough. Destiny had decided that Clarke could not lose. Johnson's handshake on the 16th brought the match to an end, and signalled the start of a well of emotion.

'I think, as a player, we all know what he can do and how good he really is,' said Johnson. 'But he's an even better person … it was a lot of emotion, obviously more for him than me. And, I don't know, I could have had my A-plus game and I'm not so sure I could have beat him. The gods were on his side. He's a great guy.'

. . . .

Europe had won the Ryder Cup for the third time in a row, but other business remained to be completed. Woosnam's team had secured an unprecedented third straight win over the Americans, a feat guaranteed once Henrik Stenson won his match. However, there were other matches in play and the Welshman eyed up the prospect that a record-making victory margin was on the cards.

Paul McGinley was playing the 17th hole, in the match ahead of Clarke, when he heard the roars from behind on the 16th. If it were possible, his smile grew larger than at any time that day. Nobody had enjoyed the atmosphere that had prevailed all around the course that Sunday as much as McGinley. He revelled in it, and as he played the 17th hole, the Dubliner—who had once been a touring professional at The K Club and who was responsible for building a new tee box out into the River Liffey that made the hole known as 'Half Moon' one of the most demanding on tour anywhere—was all-square in his match with JJ Henry.

McGinley had gotten off to a storming start against Henry. He won the second hole in par and then holed a 10-foot birdie putt on the third to be two-up. The home crowds lifted him as he walked from green to tee. McGinley was still two-up as he made his way to the ninth tee. But it was around the turn that he suffered a change in fortunes. Henry won the ninth with par, after McGinley missed from 12-feet, and then claimed the 10th in birdie with a five-foot putt to make the match all-square. Henry won his third hole in a row when claiming the 11th, where McGinley's 12-foot birdie putt shaved the hole, but the Irishman was to get matters back to all-square by taking the 13th with a winning par.

The two were toe to toe, par for par, over the stretch down by the Liffey but they couldn't be separated. Only three of the 12 singles went as far as the 18th hole on that final day. In the top match, Montgomerie had finished off Toms on the hole known as

'Hooker's Graveyard' and McGinley, who had an unbeaten record in singles in the Ryder Cup, looked to do the same. Lee Westwood would also need to take his match to the death. But McGinley looked set to finish off the job. He had put his third shot close to the hole, for what would effectively be a tap-in birdie when it came his turn to putt. Before that, Henry faced a difficult, breaking 30-footer of his own.

It was then that McGinley noticed an unwelcome guest intruding on their game. A male 'streaker' had emerged from behind the ropes and had ventured onto the edge of the green.

'Get away, you clown,' said McGinley. And, as he said the words, he realised there was only one thing to do. He approached Des Smyth, the European vice-captain, for advice. He was told that the decision was his own. If he wanted to concede a 30-foot putt, that was his call. McGinley knew what he wanted to do. The Irishman walked down to Henry, who was preparing to take his putt, and conceded it to him. Halved match.

'I felt it was the right thing to do,' said McGinley. 'There were those who felt the streaker should have been pushed into the lake and told to go swimming for Tiger's nine-iron.'

But McGinley's gesture, not unique in the Ryder Cup—Payne Stewart having done similar in the 1999 match at Brookline with Colin Montgomerie—was taken in the spirit it was given.

Henry, who had played three and halved three matches in his Ryder Cup debut, appreciated the grand gesture.

'I think it shows what the spirit of this competition is all about, what a gentleman Paul is ... of course, we did have some extracurricular activities going on at the same time. We had a great match, neck-and-neck virtually the entire way. (But) I tip my hat to him, it was a remarkable thing he did.'

McGinley walked off the 18th green, that permanent smile in place. He wanted to know one thing.

'Did Darren hole the winning putt?' he asked.

He was told that Stenson had.

McGinley nodded.

But it wasn't about one man, it was about the team. McGinley, of all players, understood that.

'Nobody understands how good this team is and how good our (European) Tour is,' said McGinley. 'For the last two years, I've been saying our European Tour is going to make this the toughest team ever [to make] because the standard is so good, the scoring is so good.'

As he stood greenside, the crowds continued to throw adulation on their home man. The player was guilty; guilty of the sin of pride. It didn't matter.

'I'm so, so proud. I'm very emotional. I'm proud not just for me and the team, but for the Irish people and the way they behaved this week, bar that clown on the last green. I'm just very, very proud. We put on a great show. All credit to Dr Smurfit and the Irish Tourism Board, but most obviously the team.'

The match was over, but the games had gone on. Padraig Harrington, playing in the final singles, hadn't played badly in the 2006 Ryder Cup, but it seemed that the gods had conspired against him. Scott Verplank had gone into the singles with a point to prove. Although a captain's pick, Tom Lehman had only given him one match—a win, as it happened—before the singles. American television analyst, Johnny Miller, had further irked the likeable Verplank by describing him during the previous day's fourballs as 'deadwood'. The feed had gone live to the US team locker room, and Verplank had heard the comment.

Verplank, although on the losing team, produced the shot of the day on that Sunday. If Harrington had suspected that the golfing gods were against him for much of the round, he was sure of it after the Par 3 14th hole. There, with the cup cut 213 yards away from the tee, Verplank proceeded to hole-out with his tee-shot, landing the ball eight feet short of the hole and then listening to the crowd's growing incredulity at greenside as the ball finished up in the cup.

'It was just a lucky shot,' ventured Verplank. 'I hit a nice looking shot that never left the flag. But, you know, to go in is pretty lucky.'

To his credit, Harrington attempted to follow him in, hitting his iron to within eight feet of the hole. But the impossible could not be expected to happen again, not in the same singles match. That hole-in-one from Verplank, the sixth in Ryder Cup history, and almost 24 hours to the hour since Paul Casey had finished his foursomes match the previous day, had put the American four up with four to play and the high-tempo singles—Verplank had four birdies and an eagle while Harrington had three birdies— eventually came to an end in the American's favour.

Verplank had gotten off to a great start by playing a wonderful iron approach to the first before rolling in the three-foot birdie putt to go one-up. Harrington brought the match back to all-square with a birdie of his own on the second, only for Verplank to respond with another birdie on the third to regain the lead. He was never to lose it again, turning two-up and increasing his lead to three holes with a winning par on the short 12th.

While the loud roars reverberating around the course were indicating one European singles win after another, Verplank stuck gamely to his task before producing his own massive roar of acclamation on the 14th where he recorded his ace.

'I was three-up at the time and trying to get the thing over. I knew I hit a good shot, was hoping it would be close … and it went in. I just turned around and told Padraig, "Well, it's your shot now." He actually hit a beautiful shot in there to eight feet and I said, that one's good. And we went on to the next hole.'

Verplank finally finished the match on the 15th hole. It gave him some personal satisfaction, gaining two wins from two matches, but the bigger picture was that the US had lost. Verplank walked off the 15th wondering why he had been utilised just twice in the contest.

· · · ·

José María Olazábal had not played a singles match in the Ryder Cup since one of the most infamous of all, his match with Justin Leonard at Brookline in 1999. It was on the 17th green at the Country Club in the upmarket suburb of Birmingham in Detroit that Ollie had watched, patiently, as his opponent holed a long and unlikely putt that prompted wild celebrations from US players, caddies and wives who, displaying the emotions of the moment, ran onto the green to congratulate Leonard.

Ollie still had a birdie putt left to halve the hole and, when the time came for him to take it, he missed; and the US had won the Ryder Cup. There were no such histrionics, no such drama, in his singles match with Phil Mickelson. On the 17th green on the Palmer Course, Olazábal had a par four, the same as Phil Mickelson. That halved hole was sufficient to give Olazábal a 2 and 1 win over the US Masters champion.

For Olazábal, the return to Ryder Cup duty had been as good as he had hoped to dream. Three matches, three wins, a 100% record. Olazábal's return to the European team after a seven year absence had been an emotional one, if not on the same level as that of Clarke's, but it had proven to be an immensely rewarding one for the Spaniard.

Olazábal got his singles match with Mickelson off to a fine start with a 20-foot birdie putt to win the third hole. It was to be a short-lived lead, as Mickelson's birdie on the tough Par 4 fifth hole levelled matters. However, the match swung Olazábal's way again on the sixth—where Mickelson ran up a double-bogey six—and the European carried that one hole lead with him all the way to the 12th, where he rolled in a 12-footer for birdie to increase his lead to two holes. Olazábal's experience then came into play. He knew that the onus was on Mickelson to be the more aggressive, to dredge up birdies from somewhere. It was not to be. The following five holes were all shared in par, and when the polite handshake came on the 17th down by the banks of the River Liffey, the roars that greeted the gesture were all to acclaim Olazábal.

'The Ryder Cup is a very special event, very unique. The more you play, the more you realise that … and especially so when the years go by,' remarked Olazábal, who increased Europe's lead to 17 ½ to 9 ½. Only one match remained on the course, and, for only the third time in the singles, it was destined to finish on the 18th hole.

The final act of Sunday's singles involved Lee Westwood, who had started to come down with flu symptoms, and Chris DiMarco, a man who didn't know when defeat was, well, defeat. The Westwood-DiMarco match was the last one to be finished on an historic day for Europe—and, for the USA too, albeit for different reasons—as the home side claimed a third straight win. Three straight defeats for the US.

That the Westwood-DiMarco match got to the 18th hole at all was a wonder. Westwood had covered the first seven holes in five-under and reached the turn five holes up on DiMarco. Even when word filtered back that all was lost, that Europe had retained the Ryder Cup, DiMarco refused to let go. Slowly, but surely, he reduced the deficit. He won the 12th. He won the 13th. He won the 16th. He won the 17th. He fist-pumped the air as if it really mattered. To him, it did.

DiMarco had come from five down to one down. But it all went horribly and anticlimactically wrong on the 18th, where the American put his ball into the lake. Still, he refused to concede defeat. DiMarco went to the drop zone and also put his next shot into the water. His plight was a sorry parody of what had happened to the USA team on that final day of singles.

Westwood won by two holes. It meant that Europe's winning margin was 18 ½ to 9 ½, identical to the record European winning margin achieved in Oakland Hills two years previously.

SEVENTEEN

Pure Genius

Co. Kildare, Ireland. Sunday Evening, 24 September, 2006.

'Where do you come from?
We come from Europe,
The mighty, mighty Europe.
Who are you? Who are you?
We're the boozy Woosie's army,
The boozy Woosie's army.'

THE PARTY HAD STARTED. UP on the balcony of the clubhouse overlooking the 18th hole, where thousands upon thousands of golf fans had assembled, Europe's players and caddies had started to enjoy the fruits of their labour. Bottles of Moet & Chandon champagne were uncorked, and, without any regard for the price of such a beverage, the bubbly contents were sprayed and swigged in equal measure. They didn't have to worry about cost or quantity. After what they'd achieved, there was an endless supply.

The chorus that the caddies conjured up for the occasion wasn't anything that Andrew Lloyd Webber would ever have produced, but 'Scotchie' and 'Wee Man' and 'Lordie' and 'Ro' and the rest of the bagmen donned curly green wigs and sang to their hearts' content. The crowd returned the compliment with a song of its own, a far more melodic tune.

'Low lie, the Fields of Athenry ...,' the traditional sporting anthem of Irish teams, came wafting upwards to the players and caddies, their wives and girlfriends, and beaming European Tour officials.

Billy Foster was there one moment, and gone the next. He had disappeared from his master's side for a very good reason. Foster, a veteran of nine Ryder Cups as a caddie, knew that Darren Clarke had a public image of imbibing in fine wines and smoking only the biggest and grandest of cigars, but that his drink of choice was an ice cold Guinness. When Foster returned to the mayhem on the veranda, he had a freshly pulled pint of stout in his hands and pushed it into the player's grasp.

Clarke didn't need to be asked twice. He took the pint and downed it in seconds, the creamy froth hugging the rim of the glass to testify to its quality. Ian Woosnam, his captain, looked at him with a hint of envy and, before he knew it, a pint was placed in his hands and he too downed the drink, slightly slower, in one go. The merriment had started in earnest.

The drinking contest was a mere sideshow. Behind the fun and games, the bond that existed between Clarke and Woosnam was greater. Clarke had wanted to play in the Ryder Cup from the time that it had been awarded to Ireland in 1997. Personal tragedy, his wife's death on 13 August, had made golf a secondary consideration in his life. But he felt that he could contribute to the team, if he was there. Woosie believed. It was Woosnam who took the courage of that conviction by giving Clarke a 'wild card' pick.

'Woosie has been great,' said Clarke. 'I can't remember an occasion where we've had 12 players playing so well. His only dilemma was who to rest and who to play. You can see from the result that he chose wisely. He's been a great captain. He's done absolutely everything perfect. And, I think, the bottom line is the score reflected that. It's pretty huge to follow up that result from Detroit a couple of years ago and to do it again.'

The high spirits on the balcony, which had become Team Europe's 19th hole, went on and on and the players, led by Sergio García and Padraig Harrington, took to hurling their shoes and whatever else they could find—buckets of golf balls, bags of tees—down to the crowds below them. Prized mementos. But, finally, the players had to go, to change out of their champagne soaked Glenmuir shirts into their delicate pink jackets, supplied by tailor Louis Copeland and from the Italian fashion house, Canali. The colour of the jackets had been specially chosen: The shade of pink highlighted breast cancer awareness.

Kitted out in those pink jackets and white turtle neck tops, the trendy Europeans made their way to the same stage constructed on the practice ground where, the previous Thursday, four long days previously, they had shared star billing with the American team. As they arrived on stage, it was, as it had been all day long on the course, to a raucous reception from the huge crowds who had stayed on for the presentation of the gold trophy with Abe Mitchell at its apex. The Ryder Cup was positioned in a place of honour in the middle of the stage.

The vanquished United States team sat to one side of the trophy, the victorious European side to the other. A vacant chair, with soft red cushioning, was positioned close by.

'That's for you, come on, sit up here,' mouthed a mischievous Colin Montgomerie to Caroline Harrington, who was with the rest of the WAGS in the front row of the VIP section below the stage. The seat actually belonged to Bertie Ahern, the Irish prime minister.

An hour had passed since Europe had won the trophy. An hour of wonderful madness had ensued. But it was time for more sober celebrations than those that had occurred on the balcony of the Palmer Clubhouse. Before he presented the trophy to the European captain, Ahern commended the contribution made by Dr Michael Smurfit in bringing the tournament to Ireland for the first time.

'It has been a great privilege for our country to host the Ryder Cup,' he said.

As Ahern presented the trophy to Woosnam, an Irish Air Corps plane flew overhead, the Irish flag trailing in its wake.

'We expected a great week in Ireland, you have made it the greatest week in history,' said Woosnam extravagantly.

The hyperbole was swallowed by the golf fans with the same gusto that, a short time previously, Woosnam had guzzled champagne and Guinness.

Tom Lehman was gracious in defeat. 'The people of this country have made me feel so special. So, from the bottom of my heart, thank you and God bless you … you have helped make this the best Ryder Cup ever,' he told the crowd.

Earlier, Montgomerie had met Lehman's father at the back of the 17th green while the inevitable unfolded.

'This is the best team Europe has ever assembled,' the elder Lehman said to the eldest playing member of the European team. 'I have to agree,' said Montgomerie. 'We're bloody good.'

· · · ·

The dozen European players who fashioned victory in the 36th Ryder Cup had performed magnificently.

'I have to tip my hat to them,' said the US captain. The 18 ½ to 9 ½ victory for Europe equalled the record winning margin claimed at Oakland Hills two years previously, but it was probably an even better team performance. Woosnam joked that he would have some words with Paul McGinley about his concession of a 30-foot putt to JJ Henry on the 18th green in their singles match that had deprived him of possibly captaining a record team. Everyone knew that gesture had symbolised the spirit of the contest.

For all that, the dejected looks on the faces of the American players that evening told another tale. Professional sportsmen don't like losing, and, for too many of them, losing in the Ryder Cup had become a habit. Could Lehman have done any more? He had prepared diligently. No US team had ever gone to the lengths, as he had, of an advance trip to a venue. He had instilled a spirit and bonding in the US team room that was eerily like that of Europe's.

Only when on the golf course had it all gone wrong, and the bottom line was that results decided the winning and losing of a contest.

How? Why? The questions came thick and fast at Lehman that evening.

'Our team gave it all that we had. We wanted to give it our very best effort, to play with heart, to have courage … but I guess the European team just played better. They played great golf, made a lot of putts. They played a phenomenal golf tournament,' said Lehman.

'Europe were a very strong team, from top to bottom. They played very inspired golf. Around the greens, they were magical. This was something truly exceptional, I was just amazed at their short game.'

Tiger Woods, of all players, detested the L-word. Losing was not something that sat comfortably into his psyche. He did emerge as the leading points scorer on the US team with three from a possible five, but his ratio in Ryder Cups had worsened. Four losses, to just one win.

'Losing doesn't sit well, nor should it. We went out there, we played, and they just outplayed us. They made more putts than we did,' he said.

But no American could put a finger on the how or the why. As Jim Furyk put it, 'Everyone wants answers. What happened? Why? What's the difference between 18 ½ points and 9 ½ points? I don't think there is a guy that can give the answer on what is different. Everyone wants to ask the question immediately after the event, what can you do? You just got slapped in the face and it is hard to come up with an answer right off the bat.

'I think it's actually a good time for reflection, you can run with it probably a million different ways ... we've obviously got outplayed in all aspects, and we've done just a horrendous job in the five Ryder Cups I've played in, four of them we've done a horrendous job on Friday and Saturday in team play. I guess if we had all the answers that were that simple, the results would probably be a little bit better for us.'

The Europeans had answered all of the questions on the golf course. Europe had won for the third time running, and the fifth time in six matches. In the modern era of the Ryder Cup, Europe were dominant. It was a stark contrast to the olden days, when Jack Nicklaus had felt compelled in the late 1970s to issue a heartfelt plea to broaden the selection process beyond Great Britain and Ireland to include continental Europe.

'There's nothing sweeter than beating the Americans,' García remarked. He spoke for every one of his team.

Woosnam had been asked to captain the team 18 months before the match at The K Club. That Sunday evening, he was proclaimed as one of the finest European captains in the event's history. He had proven to be a leader of men, and innovative with it. He had overseen the making of the motivational video that had the Rudyard Kipling poem as its focal point. He had brought sports psychologist Jamil Qureshi in as part of his back-room team. One of the bonding sessions overseen by Qureshi involved players sketching Colin Montgomerie. Sergio García, it seemed, did a particularly good one of Monty. It had him wearing an Afro hairstyle. Bonding.

'To walk away with the same record (score) Bernhard Langer has, is unbelievable. It is a dream come true for me. I've been worried for the past 18 months because it is an unbelievable responsibility to be a captain ... and I think we have the strength in depth for a long time to come, and I think the future of the Ryder Cup is going to look great for Europe,' Woosnam said as he looked back at his achievement.

The pink jackets that the European players wore that Sunday evening were not just a token gesture: Woosnam, on behalf of all the team, dedicated the win to Heather Clarke.

The party went on long into the night in the five-star K Club hotel.

'Heather would have been in the middle of all this, if she were here,' remarked Paul McGinley. He turned to Darren Clarke.

'Big D, you've been great this week. We're so proud of the way that you've handled everything, but the way you've played as well. All credit (to you), we're one big family (on tour) and we miss Heather dearly.'

In the European entertainments room in the hotel, the champagne flowed. Lee Westwood hadn't felt too well, suffering from a chest infection, and had gone to bed at 8.45pm. An hour later, his phone rang. His presence was demanded back downstairs. When he arrived, the room had been swelled by the arrival of many gatecrashers to the party. Even with tight security, some people had inveigled a way in. Westwood, after a few hot Irish whiskies and cloves to keep away the effects of illness, managed to stay partying until five in the morning.

As for the drinking contest? 'Woosie is an amateur when it comes to drinking Guinness. He's a good Ryder Cup captain, and he should leave it at that,' joked Clarke.

The Americans, too, let their hair down. The karaoke machine was fully booked and utilised until dawn broke. Mickelson and Woods played table tennis until late. If Lehman had achieved one thing from the week, it was that the team bonded. That would be his legacy. It's just that Woosnam's team bonded, and played, that much better.

EIGHTEEN

Back to Normality

Hertfordshire, England. September 2006.

TIGER WOODS RETURNED TO WINNING ways the week after the Ryder Cup. Thomas Bjørn admitted he hadn't carried out his boycott of the television and that, yes, he had delightedly watched the drama unfold at The K Club. Darren Clarke got back to his parental duties.

On the eve of the WGC-American Express championship at The Grove, just north of London, Clarke's second child, Conor, celebrated his sixth birthday. It was an occasion that was marked by a party that had a travelling zoo—complete with monkeys, snakes and centipedes—as the entertainment.

'I'm not into animals like that, but he is. About four times during the party, Conor broke out into smiles that were worth a million Ryder Cups.'

Clarke had put the Ryder Cup in context. It was only a golf tournament.

Of the 24 players who played in the Ryder Cup, 21 of them made the short airline journey across the Irish Sea from Dublin to London. Paul McGinley was the only European player not to play. He had slipped outside the top 50 in the official world golf rankings in the critical fortnight before the Ryder Cup and had failed to qualify for the team. Two Americans were absent. Phil Mickelson decided that he had played enough golf for the year.

Vaughn Taylor, like McGinley, had not got a sufficiently high world ranking.

Tom Lehman, the US Ryder Cup captain, also made the trip. But he didn't play. On the day before the AmEx started, the death occurred in America of the legendary Byron Nelson. Lehman made his excuses, left and headed home to the funeral. There was only one place for him to be in such times.

Many of those who made it to The Grove, outside Watford, confessed to post-Ryder Cup wear and tear. Some just felt that they had been away from home too long.

'What I miss most is my kids. I'm not saying I want to go hop on a plane and leave. But three weeks away? I'm slightly miserable to say the least,' said Furyk.

Some of the Europeans were under the weather, and it wasn't just because the celebrations on that Sunday night had gone on late into the night, and until the dawn chorus had sounded. In fact, the Americans spent just as long partying as the victors. Clarke was one of those who suffered flu symptoms in London. His body told him it'd had enough. But he played. One of the reasons was that he had been paired with Tiger Woods for the first two rounds.

Padraig Harrington was another who struggled to readjust to playing as an individual rather than as part of a team.

'I'm surprisingly unmotivated and struggling to go out and play golf,' he said. 'But I think if I had taken the week off I would not have got out of bed.'

Harrington had more reason than most to have suffered a comedown. For over a year in the run-up to the Ryder Cup, he had been the official face of the Ryder Cup in Ireland. His image had appeared in magazines and on television advertisements *ad nauseam* in the months running up to the match. His friends had constantly joked to him that they couldn't go into the public toilets in Dublin Airport but for his face staring back at them from an advertising poster over a urinal.

'There'd been such a big build-up all year, for the past six years in fact. It was a relief (to win) as I didn't want to lose the Ryder Cup in Ireland.'

At the post-match Ryder Cup press conference on the Sunday night at The K Club, Ian Woosnam had mentioned how proud he had been of his team, from one to 12. At that, Harrington, grin on face, had put up his hand. It was a self-depreciating gesture. On paper, he had only secured one half-point from five. But he had contributed immensely in the team room; and his play had been much better than his scores indicated.

'I did what I could. Looking back, I didn't play as well as I could the first morning (fourballs). But, after that, I stuck to my guns and I've no regrets at all about it. I came up against it in a few matches and I didn't hole the putts at the right time. Whatever way you want to look at it, I did as well as I could have in that week.

'As long as the team wins, it doesn't matter who gets the points. It would be no consolation if I won five out of five and the team lost. It would be very disappointing if I only got half a point and the team lost by half a point or a point. I might have been gutted over that. And, to be honest, I am not even gutted (at getting half a point). I honestly couldn't have done any more. I couldn't have tried any harder, or worked any harder. I couldn't have been any more disciplined, or had a better attitude. All those things I was good at last week so I can't look back and have any complaints at all,' said Harrington.

One effect of the Ryder Cup in Ireland that stayed with Harrington was not just the victory achieved, but the number of American players who, in the days after the match, repeatedly approached him to commend the Irish crowds. As Woods had put it to him:

'The fans were incredible, I think the best I've ever seen. They were the most fair, the most appreciative that I've ever seen in the Ryder Cup matches.'

Harrington had not won a golf tournament for over 15 months when he played in the Ryder Cup at The K Club. Two weeks later, just as he had done after the Ryder Cup at the Belfry in 2002, he went out and won the Dunhill Links Championship, played over the three links courses of St Andrews (Old Course), Kingsbairns and Carnoustie.

Woods took an even shorter time to get over his post-Ryder Cup blues, if they existed. He proved immune to any lingering effects of the US team's defeat at The K Club. A week earlier, he had sat stony faced beside Lehman as his captain expressed in public how proud he had been of his team in defeat. The hurt of another Ryder Cup defeat sank into the core of Woods' being, but he had moved on. Quickly.

Unburdened from team responsibilities, Woods reiterated the stark fact that when thrown into individual combat, there was simply nobody better, as he cruised to an eight shot winning margin over England's Ian Poulter and Australia's Adam Scott.

Woods' individual superiority since he won the British Open in July had been nothing short of astounding. That win at The Grove provided him with a sixth straight win (officially) on the PGA Tour, although Woods himself insisted the winning streak had ended when he lost his first round match in the World Matchplay at Wentworth the week before the Ryder Cup. For good measure, Woods also included that loss at The K Club as confirmation that the streak had ended. The simple fact remained, however, that since reclaiming the claret jug at Hoylake, his bank balance from tournament prize money had increased by just over $7 million, which represented an average of $4,377 for every stroke he had hit in that unbeaten sequence.

Chris DiMarco, his Ryder Cup team-mate, didn't have anything like the year that Woods had in terms of winning. But he could empathise with him. Woods' father, Earl, had died in

May; DiMarco's mother, Norma, had died in June. It gave them a common bond.

But everyone at the 2006 match at The K Club identified with Darren Clarke. How could you comprehend losing a young wife, the mother of your two young children? The crowds, especially, took him to their hearts; his team-mates embraced him and brought him into the zone of comfort as much as they could in the team-room; and the American players extended the hands of friendship.

All of their actions showed that the Ryder Cup was not a matter of life and death; it was simply a golf tournament. It was a darn good one; but it was just a tournament nonetheless.

The 2006 Ryder Cup Teams

US Team	US Players' Caddies
Tom Lehman	---Captain---
Tiger Woods	Steve Williams
Phil Mickelson	Jim McKay
Jim Furyk	Mike 'Fluff' Cowan
Chad Campbell	Judd Burkett
David Toms	Scott Gneiser
Chris DiMarco	Ryan Rue
Vaughn Taylor	Adam Hayes
J.J. Henry	Matt Hauser
Zach Johnson	Damon Green
Brett Wetterich	Patrick Tarrant
Stewart Cink	Frank Williams
Scott Verplank	Scott Tway

European Team	European Players' Caddies
Ian Woosnam	---Captain---
Darren Clarke	Billy Foster
Paul Casey	Craig Connelly
Luke Donald	Christian Donald
Sergio Garcia	Glen Murray
Padraig Harrington	Ronan Flood
David Howell	Michael Doran
Robert Karlsson	Garreth Lord
Paul McGinley	Darren Reynolds
Colin Montgomerie	Alastair McLean
Jose Maria Olazabal	Philip Morby
Henrik Stenson	Grant Berry
Lee Westwood	John Graham

Ryder Cup Results 1927 – 2004

2004 *Oakland Hills, Michigan*: US 9½, Europe 18½.

2002 *The Belfry, Birmingham, England*: Europe 15½, US 12½.

1999 *Brookline, Massachusetts*: US 14½, Europe 13½.

1997 *Valderrama, Spain*: Europe 14½, US 13½.

1995 *Oak hill, Rochester, New York*: US 13½, Europe 14½.

1993 *The Belfry, Birmingham, England*: Europe 13, US 15.

1991 *Kiawah Island, South Carolina*: US 14½, Europe 13½.

1989 *The Belfry, Birmingham, England*: Europe 14, US 14.

1987 *Muirfield Village, Columbus, Ohio*: US 13, Europe 15.

1985 *The Belfry, Birmingham, England*: Europe 16½, US 11½.

1983 *Palm Beach Gardens, Florida*: US 14½, Europe 13½.

1981 *Walton Heath, Surrey, England*: Europe 9½, US 18½.

1979 *Greenbrier, West Virginia*: US 17, Europe 11.

1977 *Royal Lytham & St. Annes, England*: Britain and Ireland 7½, US 12½.

1975 *Laurel Valley, Pennsylvania*: US 21, Britain and Ireland 11.

1973 *Muirfield, Scotland*: Britain and Ireland 13, US 19.

1971 *Old Warson, St. Louis, Missouri*: US 18½, Britain and Ireland 13½.

1969 *Royal Birkdale, Southport, England*: Britain and Ireland 16, US 16.

1967 *Champions Club, Houston, Texas*: US 23½, Britain and Ireland 8½.

1965 *Royal Birkdale, Southport, England*: Britain and Ireland 12½, US 19½.

1963 *East Lake, Atlanta, Georgia*: US 23, Britain and Ireland 9.

1961 *Royal Lytham & St. Annes, England*: Britain and Ireland 9½, US 14½.

1959 *El Dorado Country Club, California*: US 8½, Britain and Ireland 3½.

1957 *Lindrick, Sheffield, England*: Britain and Ireland 7½, US 4½.

1955 *Thunderbird Club, California*: US 8, Britain and Ireland 4.

1953 *Wentworth, Surrey, England*: Britain and Ireland 5½, US 6½.

1951 *Pinehurst, North Carolina*: US 9½, Britain and Ireland 2½.

1949 *Ganton, Scarborough, England*: Britain and Ireland 5, US 7.

1947 *Portland, Oregon*: US 11, Britain and Ireland 1.

1937 *Southport and Ainsdale, England*: Britain 4, US 8.

1935 *Ridgewood, New Jersey*: United States 9, Britain 3.

1933 *Southport and Ainsdale, England*: Britain 6½, US 5½.

1931 *Scioto Club, Columbus, Ohio*: US 9, Britain 3.

1929 *Moortown, Leeds, England*: Britain 7, US 5.

1927 *Worcester, Massachusetts*: US 9½, Britain 2½.

The 2006 Ryder Cup Statistics

Europe: 18½ US: 9½

Day One: 22 September – Europe 5 US 3

FOURBALLS

Harrington & Montgomerie lost to Woods & Furyk; 1 Hole.
Casey & Karlsson halved with Cink & Henry.
García & Olazábal beat Toms & Wetterich; 3&2.
Clarke & Westwood beat Mickelson & DiMarco; 1 Hole.

EU & US denote European or US advantage. AS denotes All Square/Level on shots.

Match 1																	US win by 1 Hole	
Hole	1	2	3	4	5	6	7	8	9	10	11	12	13	14	15	16	17	18
Par	4	4	3	5	4	4	4	3	4	5	4	3	4	3	4	5	4	5
Harrington	4				4	4		3	4	5			4			4		
Montgomerie		4	3	4			4				4	3		2	4		4	4
Woods	5		3			4	5	2			3	2		3	4	5		
Furyk	3	4		4	5			3	5			4					4	4
Match Progress	US 1up	US 1up	US 1up	US 1up	AS	AS	EU 1up	AS	US 1up	US 1up	US 2up	US 3up	US 3up	US 2up	US 2up	US 1up	US 1up	US 1up

Match 2   EUR – US, A/S

Hole	1	2	3	4	5	6	7	8	9	10	11	12	13	14	15	16	17	18
Par	4	4	3	5	4	4	4	3	4	5	4	3	4	3	4	5	4	5
Casey	4	4		3	4		5	3		5				3	4	4	4	4
Karlsson			2			4	4		3	4	4	3	4					
Cink	4			4	4	4		4	4			2				4		
Henry	4	3	3				5	3			3	2	4		3	5		4
Match Progress		US		EU	EU	EU	EU	EU	EU	EU	EU	EU	EU		US			
	AS	1up	AS	1up	1up	1up	2up	2up	3up	3up	2up	1up	1up	AS	1up	AS	AS	AS

Match 3   EUR Win, 3&2

Hole	1	2	3	4	5	6	7	8	9	10	11	12	13	14	15	16	17	18
Par	4	4	3	5	4	4	4	3	4	5	4	3	4	3	4	5	4	5
García	3		3	4		3	4	3			3	3		3	3	4		
Olazábal	4	3			4			3	5			4						
Toms		3	3	4	4	3	4		4			3	3	5	3	4	4	
Wetterich	4							3		4								
Match Progress	EU	EU	EU	EU	EU	EU	EU	EU	EU	EU	EU	EU	EU	EU	EU	EU		
	1up	1up	1up	1up	1up	1up	1up	1up	2up	1up	1up	1up	2up	2up	3up	3up		

Match 4																	EUR Win, by 1 Hole	
Hole	1	2	3	4	5	6	7	8	9	10	11	12	13	14	15	16	17	18
Par	4	4	3	5	4	4	4	3	4	5	4	3	4	3	4	5	4	5
Clarke	3	4		4				3			4	3	3			4	4	4
Westwood	4		3	5		4	4		4	4				3	4			
Mickelson	4	4	3	4	4	4			4			3		3	4	5		
DiMarco							4	3		5	3		3				4	4
Match Progress	EU	EU	EU							EU						EU	EU	EU
	1up	1up	1up	AS	AS	AS	AS	AS	AS	1up	AS	AS	AS	AS	AS	1up	1up	1up

FOURSOMES

Harrington & McGinley halved with Campbell & Johnson.

Howell & Stenson halved with Cink & Toms.

Westwood & Montgomerie halved with Mickelson & DiMarco.

Donald & García beat Woods & Furyk; 2 Holes.

Match 1																	EUR – US, A/S	
Hole	1	2	3	4	5	6	7	8	9	10	11	12	13	14	15	16	17	18
Par	4	4	3	5	4	4	4	3	4	5	4	3	4	3	4	5	4	5
Harrington / McGinley	5	4	2	5	4	4	4	3	5	5	4	3	4	4	4	5	3	5
Campbell / Johnson	3	4	3	5	4	5	4	3	3	5	5	3	4	4	5	4	3	4
Match Progress	US	US				EU	EU	EU			EU	EU	EU	EU	EU	EU	EU	
	1up	1up	AS	AS	AS	1up	1up	1up	AS	AS	1up	1up	1up	1up	2up	1up	1up	AS

Match 2 EUR – US, A/S

Hole	1	2	3	4	5	6	7	8	9	10	11	12	13	14	15	16	17	18
Par	4	4	3	5	4	4	4	3	4	5	4	3	4	3	4	5	4	5
Howell / Stenson	4	4	2	4	4	4	4	3	4	4	4	3	4	3	5	4	4	5
Cink / Toms	4	3	3	5	3	4	4	3	4	5	4	3	4	3	3	4	4	5
Match Progress		US		EU						EU	EU	EU	EU	EU				
	AS	1up	AS	1up	AS	AS	AS	AS	AS	1up	1up	1up	1up	1up	AS	AS	AS	AS

Match 3 EUR – US, A/S

Hole	1	2	3	4	5	6	7	8	9	10	11	12	13	14	15	16	17	18
Par	4	4	3	5	4	4	4	3	4	5	4	3	4	3	4	5	4	5
Westwood / Montgomerie	4	3	3	4	5	5	3	3	4	5	4	3	3	4	4	5	4	4
Mickelson / DiMarco	3	4	3	5	4	4	4	3	4	5	4	3	5	3	4	4	4	5
Match Progress	US			EU		US							EU			US	US	
	1up	AS	AS	1up	AS	1up	AS	AS	AS	AS	AS	AS	1up	AS	AS	1up	1up	AS

Match 4																	EUR win, by 2 Holes
Hole	1	2	3	4	5	6	7	8	9	10	11	12	13	14	15	16	17	18
Par	4	4	3	5	4	4	4	3	4	5	4	3	4	3	4	5	4	5
Donaldson / Garc Garcia	4	4	4	4	3	5	4	3	4	5	5	2	4	3	4	4	3	5
Wood / Furyk	6	4	3	5	4	4	4	3	4	6	4	3	3	2	4	4	4	6
Match Progress	EU	EU		EU	EU	EU	EU	EU	EU	EU	EU	EU	EU				EU	EU
	1up	1up	AS	1up	2up	1up	1up	1up	1up	2up	1up	2up	1up	AS	AS	AS	1up	2up

Day Two: 23 September – Europe 5 US 3

FOURBALLS

Casey & Karlsson halved with Cink & Henry.
García & Olazábal beat Mickelson & DiMarco; 3&2.
Clarke & Westwood beat Woods & Furyk; 3&2.
Stenson & Harrington lost to Verplank & Johnson; 2&1.

Match 1 EUR – USA, A/S

Hole	1	2	3	4	5	6	7	8	9	10	11	12	13	14	15	16	17	18
Par	4	4	3	5	4	4	4	3	4	5	4	3	4	3	4	5	4	5
Casey			3	4			4	2				3		3		4	4	4
Karlsson	4	3			4	5			4	5	4		4		4			
Cink	4		3	5	4			3		4	4	3		3	4			
Henry		4			4	4		4					4			3	3	5
Match Progress		EU	EU	EU	EU	EU	EU	EU	EU	EU	EU	EU	EU	EU	EU		US	
	AS	1up	1up	2up	2up	1up	1up	2up	2up	1up	1up	1up	1up	1up	1up	AS	1up	AS

Match 2 EUR win, 3&2

Hole	1	2	3	4	5	6	7	8	9	10	11	12	13	14	15	16	17	18
Par	4	4	3	5	4	4	4	3	4	5	4	3	4	3	4	5	4	5
García	4	3	3				3						3	4	4			
Olazábal				4	4	4	4	2		4	4	3	4					
Mickelson				5	4	4		3	4	5		3	4	2				
DiMarco	4	4	2				4				4				4	4		
Match Progress		EU		EU	EU	EU	EU	EU	EU	EU	EU	EU	EU	EU	EU	EU		
	AS	1up	AS	1up	1up	1up	1up	2up	3up	4up	4up	4up	4up	3up	3up	3up		

Match 3   EUR win, 3&2

Hole	1	2	3	4	5	6	7	8	9	10	11	12	13	14	15	16	17	18
Par	4	4	3	5	4	4	4	3	4	5	4	3	4	3	4	5	4	5
Clarke		4	3	4	3	4	4				3	3	4		4	4		
Westwood	3							3	4	5				2				
Woods			3	5		4				5	4	3	4	3				
Furyk	3	4			4		4	3	4						3	4		
Match Progress				EU	EU	EU	EU	EU	EU	EU	EU	EU	EU	EU	EU	EU		
	AS	AS	AS	1up	2up	2up	2up	2up	2up	2up	3up	3up	3up	4up	3up	3up		

Match 4   US win, 2&1

Hole	1	2	3	4	5	6	7	8	9	10	11	12	13	14	15	16	17	18
Par	4	4	3	5	4	4	4	3	4	5	4	3	4	3	4	5	4	5
Stenson	4	3	3			4		4	4	5	4	3	4					
Harrington				4	3		4							3	3	4	4	
Verplank			3			5	4	3	4					3				
Johnson	3	3		4	3					4	4	3	4		3	5	3	
Match Progress	US	US	US	US	US			US	US	US	US	US	US	US	US	US	US	
	1up	1up	1up	1up	1up	AS	AS	1up	1up	2up	2up	2up	2up	2up	2up	1up	2up	

FOURSOMES

García & Donald beat Mickelson & Toms; 2 &1.

Montgomerie & Westwood halved with Taylor & Campbell.

Casey & Howell beat Cink & Johnson; 5&4.

Harrington & McGinley lost to Woods & Furyk; 3 & 2.

Match 1 — EUR win, 2&1

Hole	1	2	3	4	5	6	7	8	9	10	11	12	13	14	15	16	17	18
Par	4	4	3	5	4	4	4	3	4	5	4	3	4	3	4	5	4	5
García / Donald	4	4	3	4	4	5	4	2	3	5	4	3	4	4	4	4	4	
Mickelson / Toms	4	4	3	4	4	5	6	2	4	5	4	2	3	4	5	5	4	
Match Progress							EU	EU	EU	EU	EU	EU			EU	EU	EU	
	AS	AS	AS	AS	AS	AS	1up	1up	2up	2up	2up	1up	AS	AS	1up	2up	2up	

Match 2 — EUR – US, A/S

Hole	1	2	3	4	5	6	7	8	9	10	11	12	13	14	15	16	17	18
Par	4	4	3	5	4	4	4	3	4	5	4	3	4	3	4	5	4	5
Montgomerie / Westwood	4	3	3	5	4	4	5	3	3	6	4	2	4	3	4	5	5	4
Campbell / Taylor	4	4	3	4	4	6	4	3	3	5	4	3	4	3	5	5	4	4
Match Progress		EU	EU			EU				US	US				EU	EU		
	AS	1up	1up	AS	AS	1up	AS	AS	AS	1up	1up	AS	AS	AS	1up	1up	AS	AS

Match 3   EUR win, 5&4

Hole	1	2	3	4	5	6	7	8	9	10	11	12	13	14	15	16	17	18
Par	4	4	3	5	4	4	4	3	4	5	4	3	4	3	4	5	4	5
Casey / Howell	5	3	2	4	4	4	4	3	4	5	4	2	4	1				
Cink / Johnson	5	4	3	5	5	4	4	3	4	5	4	4	4	1				
Match Progress		EU	EU	EU	EU	EU	EU	EU	EU	EU	EU	EU	EU	EU				
	AS	1up	2up	3up	4up	4up	4up	4up	4up	4up	4up	5up	5up	5up				

Match 4   US win, 3&2

Hole	1	2	3	4	5	6	7	8	9	10	11	12	13	14	15	16	17	18
Par	4	4	3	5	4	4	4	3	4	5	4	3	4	3	4	5	4	5
Harrington / McGinley	4	4	2	5	6	4	4	2	5	5	3	2	5	3	4	5		
Furyk / Woods	4	4	2	4	4	4	4	3	4	5	3	3	4	3	3	5		
Match Progress				US	US	US	US	US	US	US	US	US	US	US	US	US		
	AS	AS	AS	1up	2up	2up	2up	1up	2up	2up	2up	1up	2up	2up	3up	3up		

Day Three: 24 September – Europe: 8 ½ US: 3 ½

SINGLES

Montgomerie beat Toms; 1 Hole.

García lost to Cink; 4&3.

Casey beat Furyk; 2&1.

Karlsson lost to Woods; 3&2.

Donald beat Campbell; 2&1.

McGinley halved with Henry.

Clarke beat Johnson; 3&2.

Stenson beat Taylor; 4&3.

Howell beat Wetterich; 5&4.

Olazábal beat Mickelson; 2&1.

Westwood beat DiMarco; 2 Holes.

Harrington lost to Verplank; 4&3.

Match 1

Singles

Tee off time: 11:15

Match 1																		EUR win, by 1 Hole
Hole	1	2	3	4	5	6	7	8	9	10	11	12	13	14	15	16	17	18
Par	4	4	3	5	4	4	4	3	4	5	4	3	4	3	4	5	4	5
Montgomerie	4	4	2	4	6	4	4	3	4	5	4	3	4	2	4	5	4	4
Toms	4	4	3	6	5	4	4	3	4	5	4	3	4	3	4	5	3	4
Match Progress		EU	EU	EU	EU	EU	EU	EU	EU	EU	EU	EU	EU	EU	EU	EU	EU	EU
	AS	AS	1up	2up	1up	1up	1up	1up	1up	1up	1up	1up	1up	2up	2up	2up	1up	1up

239

Match 2
Singles
Tee off time: 11:27

Match 2																	US win, 4&3	
Hole	1	2	3	4	5	6	7	8	9	10	11	12	13	14	15	16	17	18
Par	4	4	3	5	4	4	4	3	4	5	4	3	4	3	4	5	4	5
García	4	4	2	5	4	5	5	3	4	5	3	3	3	3	3			
Cink	3	3	3	4	3	4	4	4	4	5	4	2	3	3	3			
Match Progress	US 1up	US 2up	US 1up	US 2up	US 3up	US 4up	US 5up	US 4up	US 4up	US 4up	US 3up	US 4up	US 4up	US 4up	US 4up			

Match 3
Singles
Tee off time: 11:39

Match 3																	EUR win, 2&1	
Hole	1	2	3	4	5	6	7	8	9	10	11	12	13	14	15	16	17	18
Par	4	4	3	5	4	4	4	3	4	5	4	3	4	3	4	5	4	5
Casey	3	4	2	6	3	4	3	3	4	4	4	3	4	2	4	4	3	
Furyk	4	4	3	5	4	4	4	4	4	4	3	3	4	2	4	3	3	
Match Progress	EU 1up	EU 1up	EU 2up	EU 1up	EU 2up	EU 2up	EU 3up	EU 4up	EU 4up	EU 4up	EU 3up	EU 3up	EU 3up	EU 3up	EU 3up	EU 2up	EU 2up	

Match 4
Singles
Tee off time: 11:51

Match 4																US win, 3&2	
Hole	1	2	3	4	5	6	7	8	9	10	11	12	13	14	15	16	17	18
Par	4	4	3	5	4	4	4	3	4	5	4	3	4	3	4	5	4	5
Karlsson	3	4	3	5	4	4	4	3	4	4	3	3	4	3	5	5		
Woods	4	3	3	4	3	5	4	3	3	6	3	3	4	3	4	4		
Match Progress	EU		US	US	US	US	US	US	US	US	US	US	US	US	US	US		
	1up	AS	AS	1up	2up	1up	1up	1up	2up	1up	1up	1up	1up	1up	2up	3up		

Match 5
Singles
Tee off time: 12:03

Match 5																EUR win, 2&1	
Hole	1	2	3	4	5	6	7	8	9	10	11	12	13	14	15	16	17	18
Par	4	4	3	5	4	4	4	3	4	5	4	3	4	3	4	5	4	5
Donald	4	4	3	5	4	4	4	3	4	5	3	3	3	3	4	5	4	
Campbell	4	4	3	5	4	4	4	3	4	5	5	5	6	3	3	4	5	
Match Progress											EU	EU	EU	EU	EU	EU	EU	
	AS	AS	AS	AS	AS	AS	AS	AS	AS	AS	1up	2up	3up	3up	2up	1u	2up	

DAY THREE

Match 6
Singles
Tee off time: 12:15

Match 6																EUR – US, A/S		
Hole	1	2	3	4	5	6	7	8	9	10	11	12	13	14	15	16	17	18
Par	4	4	3	5	4	4	4	3	4	5	4	3	4	3	4	5	4	5
McGinley	4	4	2	5	5	4	4	3	5	5	5	3	4	3	4	5	4	4
Henry	4	5	3	5	3	5	4	3	4	4	3	3	5	3	4	5	4	4
Match Progress		EU	EU	EU	EU	EU	EU	EU	EU		US	US						
	AS	1up	2up	2up	1up	2up	2up	2up	1up	AS	1up	1up	AS	AS	AS	AS	AS	AS

Match 7
Singles
Tee off time: 12:27

Match 7																EUR win, 3&2		
Hole	1	2	3	4	5	6	7	8	9	10	11	12	13	14	15	16	17	18
Par	4	4	3	5	4	4	4	3	4	5	4	3	4	3	4	5	4	5
Clarke	4	4	3	4	4	4	4	3	4	4	4	2	5	3	4	5		
Johnson	4	4	3	5	3	5	L	3	4	5	4	3	4	3	4	5		
Match Progress				EU		EU	EU	EU	EU	EU	EU	EU	EU	EU	EU	EU		
	AS	AS	AS	1up	AS	1up	2up	2up	2up	3up	3up	4up	3up	3up	3up	3up		

Match 8
Singles
Tee off time: 12:39

Match 8																		EUR win, 4&3
Hole	1	2	3	4	5	6	7	8	9	10	11	12	13	14	15	16	17	18
Par	4	4	3	5	4	4	4	3	4	5	4	3	4	3	4	5	4	5
Stenson	4	4	3	4	4	3	3	3	4	5	4	3	4	3	4			
Taylor	3	4	3	4	4	6	4	3	5	5	4	4	4	4	4			
Match Progress	US	US	US	US	US		EU	EU	EU	EU	EU	EU	EU	EU	EU			
	1up	1up	1up	1up	1up	AS	1up	1up	2up	2up	2up	3up	3up	4up	4up			

Match 9
Singles
Tee off time: 12:51

Match 9																		EUR win, 5&4
Hole	1	2	3	4	5	6	7	8	9	10	11	12	13	14	15	16	17	18
Par	4	4	3	5	4	4	4	3	4	5	4	3	4	3	4	5	4	5
Howell	4	4	3	4	4	4	4	3	4	5	3	2	3	2				
Wetterich	4	4	3	5	4	4	6	3	3	5	4	3	4	3				
Match Progress				EU	EU	EU	EU	EU	EU	EU	EU	EU	EU	EU				
	AS	AS	AS	1up	1up	1up	2up	2up	1up	1up	2up	3up	4up	5up				

Day Three

Match 10
Singles
Tee off time: 13:03

Match 10																EUR win, 2&1		
Hole	1	2	3	4	5	6	7	8	9	10	11	12	13	14	15	16	17	18
Par	4	4	3	5	4	4	4	3	4	5	4	3	4	3	4	5	4	5
Olazábal	4	4	2	4	4	4	4	2	4	5	4	2	4	3	4	5	4	
Mickelson	4	4	3	4	3	6	4	2	4	5	4	L	4	3	4	5	4	
Match			EU	EU		EU	EU	EU	EU	EU	EU	EU	EU	EU	EU	EU	EU	
Progress	AS	AS	1up	1up	AS	1up	1up	1up	1up	1up	1up	2up	2up	2up	2up	2up	2up	

Match 11
Singles
Tee off time: 13:15

Match 11																EUR win, by 2 Holes		
Hole	1	2	3	4	5	6	7	8	9	10	11	12	13	14	15	16	17	18
Par	4	4	3	5	4	4	4	3	4	5	4	3	4	3	4	5	4	5
Westwood	3	4	2	4	4	3	3	3	5	5	4	4	5	3	4	5	4	W
DiMarco	4	5	2	6	4	4	4	3	5	5	4	2	4	3	4	4	3	L
Match	EU	EU	EU	EU	EU	EU	EU	EU	EU	EU	EU	EU	EU	EU	EU	EU	EU	EU
Progress	1up	2up	2up	3up	3up	4up	5up	5up	5up	5up	5up	4up	3up	3up	3up	2up	1up	2up

Match 12
Singles
Tee off time: 13:27

Match 12																	US win, 4&3	
Hole	1	2	3	4	5	6	7	8	9	10	11	12	13	14	15	16	17	18
Par	4	4	3	5	4	4	4	3	4	5	4	3	4	3	4	5	4	5
Harrington	4	3	3	5	3	4	4	3	4	5	4	4	4	2	4			
Verplank	3	4	2	5	3	4	3	3	4	5	4	3	4	1	4			
Match Progress	US 1up	AS	US 1up	US 1up	US 1up	US 1up	US 2up	US 2up	US 2up	US 2up	US 2up	US 3up	US 3up	US 4up	US 4up			

2006 Ryder Cup Individual Points Totals

Europe	Played	Won	Lost	Halved	Points
S. García	5	4	1	0	4
L. Westwood	5	3	0	2	4
D. Clarke	3	3	0	0	3
L. Donald	3	3	0	0	3
J. M. Olazábal	3	3	0	0	3
P. Casey	4	2	0	2	3
D. Howell	3	2	0	1	2 ½
C. Montgomerie	4	1	1	2	2
H. Stenson	3	1	1	1	1 ½
P. McGinley	3	0	1	2	1
R. Karlsson	3	0	1	2	1
P. Harrington	5	0	4	1	½

USA	Played	Won	Lost	Halved	Points
T. Woods	5	3	2	0	3
S. Cink	5	1	1	3	2 ½
J. Furyk	5	2	3	0	2
S. Verplank	2	2	0	0	2
Z. Johnson	4	1	2	1	1½
JJ Henry	3	0	0	3	1 ½
C.Campbell	3	0	1	2	1
V. Taylor	2	0	1	1	½
C. DiMarco	4	0	3	1	½
D. Toms	4	0	3	1	½
P. Mickelson	5	0	4	1	½
B. Wetterich	2	0	2	0	0

INDEX

T

Taylor, Vaughn 13, 27, 63, 80, 94, 99, 102, 103, 110, 160, 186, 187, 197, 204, 205, 224
The K Club 12-14, 23, 26, 40-41, 46, 49, 51, 54, 63, 65-66, 68-72, 75-76, 85, 90, 92-93,
        107-109, 119, 121-122, 124-125, 129, 135, 137, 141, 143-144, 149, 153, 178, 189,
        194, 198, 203, 208, 220, 221, 223, 225, 226-227
Tinning, Iben 184
Toms, David 94, 102, 103, 110, 147, 156, 157, 163-165, 186, 196, 197, 200, 203, 209
Torrance, Bob 20, 21, 71, 162
Torrance, Sam 115, 185

V

Vanstiphout, Jos 41
Verplank, Scott 104-106, 110, 133, 146, 160, 180-181, 197, 199, 210-212

W

Wall, Anthony 42, 69
Walton, Philip 143, 144
Watson, Tom 87, 107
Westwood, Lee 69, 89, 113, 116, 118-120, 133, 148, 152, 158-161, 166, 169-170, 173-
        174, 178-180, 187, 191, 197, 209, 213-214, 221
Wetterich, Brett 13, 63, 94, 99, 102, 103, 110, 131, 133, 147, 156, 157, 197, 203, 204
Williams, Steve 83, 136, 199
Wilson, Dean 92, 93, 94
Wooden, John 107
Woods, Earl 29, 37, 38, 39, 40, 76, 83, 85, 226
Woods, Elin. *See* Nordegren, Elin
Woods, Tiger 27-29, 32-38, 47, 53-54, 56, 76-79, 81-87, 93-96, 98-103, 107-110, 123,
        131-133, 135-138, 146-147, 151-154, 163, 165-168, 171, 174, 178-180, 182, 186-
        188, 197-199, 202, 206, 219, 223-226
Woosnam, Ian 12-15, 18, 41, 46, 48, 53, 62, 64-65, 67, 70, 73, 90, 98, 112-113, 115,
        116, 117-121, 124-126, 128-130, 133, 143, 145-149, 151, 154-156, 160, 161, 163-
        164, 168-169, 171-174, 182-183, 185, 189, 191-195, 197, 200, 205-208, 216, 218,
        220-222, 225